KU-359-129

POLITICS AND PERSONS

POLITICS AND PERSONS

FATHER ST. JOHN B. GROSER

With a foreword by R. H. Tawney

SCM PRESS
56 Bloomsbury Street, London, W.C.1

First published May 1949

*Distributed in Canada by our exclusive agents
The Macmillan Company of Canada Limited
70 Bond Street, Toronto*

*Made and Printed in Great Britain
at the Stanhope Press, Rochester,
by Staples Press Limited*

CONTENTS

FOREWORD

BY

R. H. Tawney

BOOKS revealing not merely the facts of urban life and work, but the human reaction to them, are not too numerous. *Politics and Persons* deserves a high place among them. Combining an unusual width of practical experience with a sensitiveness of insight given to few, the author is concerned less with the material conditions of a much-tried population than with the mentality born of the revolt against them. East London is his base; but he sees in the plight of his parish in the inter-war years a picture in miniature of the needs of the nation, and, while his feet are firmly planted in the sticky clay of Stepney, surveys from his observation-post horizons beyond it. Thus his reflections on the lessons to be learned from struggles in which he did not play a passive part have a significance transcending the particular environment which supplies their setting. The conditions described in his pages appear to him the symptom of a more profound disorder. He offers not merely a narrative, but a diagnosis and a prescription.

On the industrial background it is needless to dwell. In the year in which Father Groser settled in East London the depression which succeeded the post-war boom still lay heavy on it. The Poplar Guardians, sent to gaol for refusing to apply in 1921 the principles of 1834, had just returned in triumph home. One in seven of British workers was unemployed; and, though few then foresaw it, a rate not far below that figure was to stand as the average over another fifteen years. The south suffered less than the north; but even in London, where, except in the dreadful early 1930's, mass unemployment was not the curse it was elsewhere, there were few families of wage-earners who, if not themselves afflicted by it, could not count relations and friends among its victims. Fear born of insecurity, with the odious inhumanities of the means test as the penalty for misfortune, was everywhere in the air. It is not surprising that the atmosphere created by it should pervade the author's opening chapters, or that he should give short shrift to the nostalgic self-deception which turns from the common inconveniences and shared deprivations of the post-war world to sigh for the exclusive felicities and securely guarded flesh-pots of the days before the deluge. Yet the impression made on his reader is not one of gloom. It is of an unquenchable vitality, which recognised the menace to its ideals and way of life, and was quick to take the challenge up. One has known communities in which, when things were at their worst, everything—trade unionism, education, political activity, collective effort and individual self-respect—seemed temporarily to go to pieces. The East End, to judge by Father Groser, was not among them. It did not escape unscathed, either in body or soul; but, thanks partly to a devoted group of leaders, with the lion-hearted Lansbury at their head, though primarily, no doubt, to the qualities of its people, it preserved throughout its sufferings a resolution which nerved it not only to wrestle with the stubborn folly in high places which needlessly aggravated them, but to display, as in the coal crisis of 1926 and later in the great depression, a moving solidarity with workers elsewhere. The two decades following the first world war were not, it appears, the interlude of sterility that at the time they sometimes seemed. The popular temper which knew the Nazi tyranny for the abomination it was, in the days when eminences and notabilities still sought excuses for it, found its sustenance in them. The unbreakable spirit which first won the war, and then provided victory with its appropriate British sequel, was hardened in the miseries of the same unhappy period.

Few persons, it is probable, are captured by creeds whose principles they have not, in some sense, already long shared. An Anglican priest converted to Socialism, not by the dialectics of the doctors, but by his flock, Father Groser met in it a temper and attitude of mind neither alien to his faith nor a mere excrescence on it. He loved what his people loved, and hated what they hated. It was natural that he should participate, as a member and a leader, in the corporate efforts and activities in which love and hate found expression. The Socialism learned from daily contact with the rank and file of the Labour Movement is apt to be marked by a native justice of moral sentiment, as well as a gusto and robustness, not always conspicuous in the doctrinal convolutions of the more intricate article elaborated by the schools. The great art of complicating the simple and obscuring the obvious, by which the authentic intellectual proves his title to that proud name, is not one which the author has felt called on to acquire. Possessing a theology, he found it needless to invent one; and his co-operative commonwealth is not of those rarefied Utopias which leave their reader feeling that Socialism, thus expounded, has an answer to every question except why any child of man should conceivably desire it. It is a home to be built by men and women for themselves, with the eccentricities, lovable and odious, of unregenerate human nature to enliven or confound it, not an enclosure for tame animals with wise keepers in command. The poison of the pre-war social order was, it seems to him, a sin of the spirit. It was its tranquil acquiescence in that manipulation of economic power for private gain of which, since it makes the mass of mankind the instruments of the ambition, convenience or caprice of a minority, the proper name is tyranny. It was, in short, a temper that tolerated the treatment of men, not as men, but as things. That denial of the dignity of man, corrupting to its supposed beneficiaries not less than to their victims, is a reversal of the true order and relations of human life with which no society even faintly imbued with a residuum of Christian values can presume to make a truce. The path towards the light is, doubtless, long and winding, but the destination is plain. It is the control of "the things and processes'' of economic life by ''persons responsible to a community of persons''.

In proclaiming freedom and fellowship as the words of salvation, Father Groser could cite honoured names, from William Morris to William Temple, to testify for him. The nemesis of a religion which loses its hold on the great commonplaces of existence is commonly not indifference, but a counter-religion. The counter-religion has not failed to come. The patient good humour of the author's reflections on British Communism is a model for imitation. Of its theoretical load of Mid-Victorian luggage he says sufficient, but not more; nor does he waste words on the gyrations either of the elderly cynics, jumping backwards and forwards through hoops with a docility that would sicken a self-respecting poodle, who masquerade as its leaders, or of the fringe of cautious sycophants who make discreet eyes at them. The fact remains that, when a system is such that those involved in it feel trapped in a vice, they do right to strive to break it, and that, in such circumstances, it is often not the worst, but the best, who answer total injustice by total self-surrender. The sincerity of devotees of that stamp, especially the younger of them, deserves the sympathetic respect which is shown it in these pages. Unfortunately, sincerity, an attribute of inquisitors and maniacs as well as of saints, is not by itself the whole armour of man. The logic of the last resort—''stone-dead hath no fellow''—turns the ethics of war—cruelty, treachery and lying—into a prescription for peace. The pretence that a despotism is not a despotism, but the servant of the people, the proletariat, the true and virtuous citizens, is the stalest trick of tyranny; nor does experience lend colour to the credulity which assumes that a dictatorship, once firmly in the saddle, will make haste to dismount. The victory of a cause thus inspired is a defeat for humanity.

If the pseudo-realism—the Machiavellism foreign to Machiavelli—which urges that the sanctified end sanctifies all means, be repudiated, what, it may be asked, remains? What remains, the writer replies, is something less dramatic than a generation of violence and counter-violence, but more civilised and less unchristian. There are countries so unfortunate, and situations so bedevilled by past follies and crimes, that the dilemma of remorseless extremes could hardly be avoided in them; and verdicts which ignore that tragic truth are neither just nor scientific. England has had her breakdowns; but, since the advent of democracy, her people, when it has known its mind, which too often it has not, has known also how to make its will prevail by methods less inhuman. The immolation of existing lives, in the name of economic progress, on the altar of an imagined future has been among the crimes of capitalism. It is not, the author urges, for Socialists to repeat it. Except to the incorrigible melodramatist, the significance of measures is a question not of the heat and smoke surrounding their enactment, but of their substance and content. If the result is to reconstruct important institutions, to transform the relations between classes, and to alter the balance of social power, then, however unspectacular the procedure employed, the much-misused term "revolutionary" may properly be applied to them.

In the dark days of the 'twenties and 'thirties it was for such a revolution by consent that Father Groser hoped. It is for the willing acceptance by all classes of the sacrifices involved in it that he pleads in his book. Politics have their own techniques; but their inevitable complexities make it more, not less, important that men should at times consider them simply and in human terms, as the art of accomplishing by collective action tasks which individuals cannot hope to achieve, or to achieve so well, by their isolated efforts. It is proper that, on that obvious aspect of the subject, the officer of a Christian society should state the truths suggested by his faith.

I

INTRODUCTORY

A FEW weeks ago a group of us were sitting round a fire discussing world affairs generally, and in particular the crisis in Britain. Naturally the conversation turned to the conditions prevailing between the wars, and I was drawn to talk about some of my experiences during the twenty-five years which I have spent in the East End. Most of the people present had been in the East End since the war, but not prior to 1939. When I had finished they unanimously pressed me to write that story for others to hear. It had in their opinion made present-day problems so much easier for them to understand that they thought it might equally help others.

But why should we bother about it all? We were all Christians. To a great many people a Christian should keep off politics. And the things we were talking about were very closely connected not only with politics, but with party politics. Let me deal with this question first of all, for it is central to much that I want to say.

If I remember rightly, the conversation at this meeting had begun by somebody reading an extract from the *Sunday Express*: "The Socialists lost their only seat at Torrington, Devon, making the council completely non-political"; and Ethel Upton had capped it by saying that when she was working with me at Watney Street a dear old lady came into the church and remarked: "What a pity the Vicar is so political!" adding as an afterthought: "The Vicar at my church is a Conservative."

"But isn't that political?" she was asked.

"Oh, no," she replied, "that's in the Prayer Book. We are told to pray for the King and his Government."

I can remember when I felt rather like that myself. It was in the days when the Socialist seemed rather an interloper in a game played by those whom we later described as Tweedledum and Tweedledee. There were, of course, even then real issues at stake, but they didn't seem to be matters of life and death, and the horrid Socialist seemed to be introducing a foreign element into it.

The first election which I can remember in England was in 1906. In those days polling was spread over several days, and so we had to wait for the newspapers every morning to see how the parties were getting on. We youngsters played something like a racehorse parlour game. We all had our horses which we moved about as the results came in, and our elders kept up a running fire of betting on the probable winner. It was great fun, for it was all so impersonal. We never thought that we were playing with people's lives.

In a lesser degree the same thing occurred with me in the opening stages of trench warfare in 1914. We had our map of Europe, with its German and Allied trenches marked with flags, which we moved backwards and forwards as the newspapers gave us directions each morning. Then I went out to France myself. There the whole thing became personal. Those flags which we moved about each morning, those "pushes" so laconically announced in the newspapers as small affairs, became for me now matters of life and death for human beings whom I knew. In the same way, it was not till I went to Poplar that this political business, in which I was before interested in a detached and theoretical way, became personal and real. It did matter how people voted. Lives were at stake. Persons were the issue.

Now, why is it that, as a young man preparing for the ministry and therefore not only a professing Christian, but spending most of my time studying theology, I should take this detached attitude, and later change it rather violently? It wasn't because I was a rather selfish person suddenly become unselfish; nor because I was not then interested in persons and suddenly became interested. Looking back now,

I can see that I was in a state of almost continuous revolt against certain class distinctions which prevented me from making friends of people who showed friendship to me. I remember the jolt I had when, as a boy at school, I was ticked off by a relation of mine for becoming too friendly with the son of a shopkeeper in the town and wanting him to stay with us. I remember, too, how later I used to think the whole servant relationship odd.

But the first inkling I had that all this class business was related to politics came about later, when I spent many of my holidays with some delightful people in Hertfordshire and enjoyed many seasons of cricket and shooting. The family boasted themselves of old yeoman stock; with a stake in that county since the Norman conquest; with a rich culture and old-world courtesy against which I find it even now difficult to write one word of criticism. I am for ever grateful that I was allowed a glimpse of that world and that phase of English life, which had in it so many good and pleasant things that have to my regret passed away. They were really a survival of feudalism.

A large estate with a big house full of servants; a good and well-stocked cellar; stables with riding and carriage horses; a couple of farms; and altogether on the estate about one hundred persons. The little church, built for the estate, seated exactly that number. Both there and in the private chapel in the house where morning prayers were said (alas, the Chaplain had departed some years before) every person who was able was expected to be present. The ladies of the house, the last of the direct line, were kindness itself. In those days, before old age pensions became a Government concern, no retainers of long standing were turned off the estate when they were too old to work, but were provided with light work and cottages. I remember so well how the ladies themselves would set out with broth and baskets of fruit from the garden to care for the sick and aged. The grace and charm of that life remains as a pleasant recollection; and I repeat my regret that so much of it is now no more.

But it was upheld at a cost. It demanded recognition by each one of a set station in life, and obedience to it with all that that involved; and, on top of that, a resolute determination by all to keep at arm's length the outside world gradually encroaching on their privacy. They clung to their horses, and hated the motor-cars and their smell as they streamed down the Great North Road. They resented McAdam's roads, which hurt the horses' feet. They were distrustful of every modern "improvement" which seemed to threaten this world that they understood and loved.

The ordering and setting out of "the carriage" each day was an event, and the drive round the estate, or the call on one of the other County families, was a ritual. To the passing carriage every person was expected to doff his cap or curtsey; and the failure to do so was met with a severe reprimand. If the footman was not sent at once to bring the offender to the waiting carriage, a sort of private "manorial" court would deal with the matter during the week. So long as the rules were obeyed, life was pleasant—at least on the surface. The rules were known, and the basis of them kept before the minds of both master and servant by the reading at least once a week in chapel of one or other of the passages in St. Paul's epistles relating to the subject.

But they could not keep the world at bay. For one thing, a new type of retainer was arising who was not content to be looked after at the expense of his freedom. I remember well how at last one man, after many agitated discussions in the drawing-room, was dismissed for being a Socialist. It was, I think, my first real introduction to politics.

Well, that world has gone. Try as they would, they could not shut out another world encroaching on them. The dismissal of that Socialist didn't end the matter; and it was not the Socialist who ended it. A few of those estates had survived the urbanisation of England, with its consequent impoverishment and depletion of her countryside and the destruction of her agriculture. But a new mechanisation, and the growth of the financial speculator, was soon to engulf them. A new class was arising, with the vices of the old redoubled, and with none of its graces. It was not till many years later that I was to become conscious of the new tyranny exercised by men who had bought up the old estates and exploited them with no sense of responsibility either to the soil or to the sons of the soil. These dear good ladies were fighting with the wrong weapons to defend something that was good. Had they but known it, the Socialist was on their side to preserve that good against the depersonalisation of man and the destruction of his roots in God and the soil.

A few years later, in 1914, I was ordained, and went to work in a parish on the dockside in Newcastle. My Vicar, Canon Carr, was a very saintly man, who had given himself without stint in what was one of the most difficult parishes in England, with narrow precipitous streets off which ran many little courts. Many of the houses had been built for master mariners or wealthy citizens a hundred or so years before, with lovely oak staircases, still remaining in my day, which led off into large commodious rooms that now housed as many as two or three families apiece.

There were a dozen or so sixpenny or ninepenny doss-houses in the parish, one of which had a long room in which hanging blankets divided bed from bed. In each such compartment a couple lived and slept. Other doss-houses were for men and women, separate or mixed according to tradition, who cooked for themselves on a common fire downstairs. Prostitution was, of course, rampant; and under the arches a woman could be had for a shilling. Some of the superior prostitutes went out to do business. I often used to wonder how many of the wealthier men in Newcastle knew that the women they bought came back in cabs in the early morning to these conditions.

That doss-house population was full of interest to me. Some time before I went there I had in company with a friend disguised myself as a tramp and tried my hand at begging and sleeping in a doss-house in order to learn their ways. Now I found myself trying to minister to this odd assortment of people. They were a cosmopolitan crowd, some of them with a cultured background "come down in the world". I remember one man who sold laces outside Newcastle station with a placard "blind" round his neck. He had lived in the same doss-house for years and had a remarkably fine library in his corner. The last time I saw him was in uniform in 1916, when he greeted me with: "They found me out!"

The prison stood in the middle of the parish, and it was there that I looked for any of our folk that were missing.

The police never came down the worst of those courts alone day or night. I remember once one who did, and I found him lying on his back with a crowd gathered round kicking him. I had to stand over him for about half an hour before he was rescued. I was in no danger, for I was a priest, and the superstition was inbred in those people that to touch a priest was to risk damnation. Even when they fought with knives, which not infrequently happened, we were in no danger. The only thing we were not expected to do was to interfere between husbands and wives. That was an unwarrantable intrusion in a family affair, which resulted as often as not in both turning on the intruder. There were many such rules and conventions which had to be learned, for that society was governed by them.

In the middle of all that children were born and bred; and one of my first tasks was to try to do something about the growing boys. I gathered about a hundred of them into a club, but fared rather badly when I tried to raise some money by interesting people outside in the general conditions in which they were being brought up. The Chief Inspector of Newcastle came one day to see me and to beg me to be careful. "We have most of the undesirables and 'wanted' people in the north of England in that area," he said; "we don't want them scattered." But since most of my boys, on leaving school hardly able to read or write, went naturally into various blind-alley jobs, and from these drifted on to swell the doss-house and prison population, I thought that it would be a good idea to interest the business people of the city in a scheme for assisting apprenticeships. It would, I knew, cost time and money, and risks of failure in many cases; but I was sure that I could save many of those boys between the ages of 14 and 21 whom I had in the club, if only I could obtain help to get some such scheme into operation.

Now, I have no doubt that I said and did many unwise things. I was a young man, with very little experience of the world, and I knew nothing about politics. But I had had my first introduction to real poverty and to the degradation which resulted from it, and the moment I tried to do something quite simple about it I found myself up against something else which seemed to me to be strangely inhuman. I thought in my ignorance that all that was needed was to make the facts known and the natural decency of people would rise to deal with the situation. But I was mistaken. I was up against something which I didn't then understand. I was receiving my first practical lesson in politics and its relation to the whole industrial and social set-up. I only know that I trod on the toes of some of the business people of Newcastle; that I was lifting the lid off a hell that stank and that was not pleasant to behold; that I was being called "political", because it was public policy to keep that underworld as far as possible out of sight and sound.

But I continued to press on, for I felt somehow that the only way in which I could help those boys and save them from what seemed to me to be the inevitable consequences of that situation was to take them out of it. I was astonished when one day the Bishop sent for me, and, after giving me a proper dressing-down, said quite angrily: "I sent you down there to save the souls of those people, not to look after their bodies. Go back and do the work you were ordained to do." I had had, of course, no intention of doing anything else, and I had no idea that I was being political.

I was in my own mind being no more political than in the affair about a hat. I was in Newcastle a few years ago preaching. A woman came up to me, and, after introducing her children to me, said: ''Do you remember me? I'm the girl you had a row about when I had no hat.'' This business of hats seems to be always cropping up, as indeed it is almost bound to do, for it is all mixed up with the serious business of courtesy and respectability. It had arisen at the Manor: it had caused some annoyance when I first refused to wear a top-hat on Sundays in that parish; it was to come up again in various ways in the East End—even up to 1939 there was a notice in the churchyard of St. George in the East: ''No dogs or women without hats allowed in''—and it arose now here.

It happened this way. One day I saw a little girl running down the street through the snow with bare feet and nothing on but a thin cotton frock. I stopped and talked to her, and found out where she lived. Later I visited her home, took some clothes, and finally persuaded her to come to church on Sunday. Knowing the custom of the place and not wanting to make her feel uncomfortable, I first took the precaution of buying her a hat. Next Sunday I found her crying after the service outside the church. She told me that she had been to church hatless and in her old clothes, because her father had pawned all the things I had given her; but that the Churchwarden had turned her out because she hadn't a hat on. Now, I need not dwell on the situation which followed, and which ended with the intervention of the Vicar, and his firm ruling that in future girls were to be allowed in church without hats if they hadn't got any.

But I was moving; moving out of a world in which I had taken for granted a whole set of things which I could no longer take for granted in the new set of circumstances to which I was being introduced. Class, respectability, custom, politics, these things somehow began to piece together into a pattern in which I didn't seem to fit. Although in my own mind I had no politics and was merely interested in persons, the affair about the hat seemed to others to be as clear an indication of my political bias as the trouble about the boys.

What would have happened had I stayed in that parish I don't know. But the war claimed me as a Chaplain to the Forces, and took me for the next three years to France, where I found myself up against a new set of problems in personal relationships which seemed more closely to demand political judgements. My inability to resolve them drove me to refuse a living and seek refuge in a curacy in Cornwall with time to read and pray about it all. And from there to Poplar, again deliberately refusing a living because I felt driven to go and try and work out this problem of human relationships in conditions similar to those in which I had first begun to face them. Perhaps again I should have stayed and faced them in the country, where they were obvious enough. John the gardener, who lived in a little cottage just up the lane with his wife and family, was one. John could hardly read or write, but he was a man with a deep fund of natural and acquired wisdom and the soul of courtesy. He was an expert gardener, with an almost uncanny eye for the right season for planting with no calendar to guide him; good with all animals; able to kill, cut up expertly, and salt down a pig; to my amateur mind there seemed little that John was not skilled at in country lore and crafts. Yet John was struggling to keep a wife and bring up a family on twenty-five shillings a week, and died of tuberculosis in a countryside which was rich. But I did not stay to face that and other country problems; I went to Poplar. I was this time determined that I would stay long enough to see if I could find my way through.

2

EARLY DAYS IN POPLAR

I WENT to Poplar in 1922, just after the Poplar Board of Guardians had come out of prison where they had been for six weeks. When they later wrote a pamphlet defending their actions, they not only called it *Guilty and Proud of It*, but prefaced it with a Biblical quotation: "Pure religion and undefiled before God and the Father is this, to visit the fatherless and widows in their affliction" (*James* 1. 27). I was going to leave it at that: but I can hear at once the critics say, "Humanism. Why did they leave out 'and to keep themselves unspotted from the world'?" George Lansbury, their leader, said of this criticism, in his book *These Things Shall Be*, that he could not make that part of the text his own, because he was so conscious of failure and sin in himself. I mention this because the thing which first struck me forcibly on coming to Poplar was the essentially religious nature of the revolt which was taking place.

To my shame I have to admit that, in my early days at Mirfield, I once refused to go and hear George Lansbury speak because I regarded him as a political agitator and a danger to the community; but he now became and remained to the day of his death one of my closest friends. "G. L." was a man with a simple and childlike faith and a real love for persons. There were many occasions when I did not agree with him. He was a pacifist, for one thing, and I was not. But he lived among us, spoke a language we all understood, and became for the whole movement a symbol and a rallying flag in many depressing years.

He once said to me: "John, I would sooner be here in the Bow Road where the unemployed can put a brick through my window when they disagree with my actions, than be in some other place far away where they can only write me a letter. It's good for me, and it's better for them.'' On another occasion, when the unemployed locked the Poplar Guardians in the Town Hall for a few hours, it was again typical of G. L. to say that he thought ''the unemployed ought to be ashamed of themselves for locking the Guardians in for a few hours only, instead of keeping them there. If the unemployed had kept the Guardians locked in, they would have shown the authorities at Whitehall that they really meant business, and thereby also shown that the Guardians had the unemployed with them in their determination to get the scales of relief they sought.'' It was that sort of attitude which endeared him to us all, including those who disagreed with many of his actions, and which made him so great a leader.

I learned much from him, and enjoyed particularly those Saturday evenings which we spent together in his house, whenever both of us were free. One of my last recollections of these evenings was just before he went off to interview Hitler after he had broken his leg, when he lay on the floor and kicked with both legs in the air, to our great amusement, in order to prove how much stronger he was.

In one of his last letters to me, in reply to one of mine asking him to explain some inconsistency, after defending himself, he added characteristically: ''There has always been all my life one great inconsistency I never defend or explain. I wanted to live, got married, had a large family . . . this has cost money, time, energy. I have worked for capitalists, and as a capitalist I lived on the backs of others, and received and spent hundreds and thousands of pounds from rich friends on the *Daily Herald*, the *Weekly* and the movement generally. This is all inconsistent. I might not have married, might have been, like Francis, a travelling friar; but those who fed me, clothed me, housed me, however poorly, would have done so with themselves in the competitive fight. There is no escape till death, and I won't die till I am forced. Hard though it is, I believe I can help better by living. Although I have spent so much of other people's money and at times have had even my own to spend, I shall die without any property or money; but rich, very rich, in the knowledge that I have been able to see the promised land. I am, however, confident, with Morris, that some day the masses, when they are wise enough to will it, will enter in and be satisfied.''

He was never one to believe that a miraculous change of conditions would suddenly make people good. In his book *These Things Shall Be* he wrote: ''I yield to no one my downright hatred of the present social order, built as it is on fraud and cunning, make-believe and humbug; but I cannot believe in any change being real unless it starts from individual men and women''; and again: ''Democracy, if it means anything at all, means voluntary co-operation. Whenever this is established it will at the outset call for more discipline, more abnegation of self, more work, more endurance, than any of us are called upon to exercise to-day.'' He called upon men and women ''to face the future full of the spirit which comes from God Himself, inspiring us and cheering us with the faith that we are not alone, but that He who said 'Lo I am with you even to the end' will never fail us, but in dark days and fair is ever near us to give us hope and strength, confidence and courage to stand before the world and proclaim our faith: 'Yea though He slay me yet will I trust Him'; and by this faith show to all the world that His life, His death, His message, is to us the real dynamic driving force by which mankind must and will be saved''.

There have been fewer sadder days in my life than the one in which G. L. told me that he could no longer make his Communion because of what he felt was the apostasy of the Church. He had, he said, put in a great deal of work on the Archbishops' Committee of Enquiry, ''to consider and report upon the ways in which the Church may best commend the teaching of Christ to those who are seeking to solve the problems of industrial life''. That Committee published in 1919 a report which is in many ways a landmark in the history of the Church of England, and would well repay careful reading and study to-day. But subsequent events led G. L. to the conclusion that, though the Church of England, when driven to it, was bound in the light of the Gospel to come to some such conclusions, she had no intention of doing anything about it, and was, in fact, becoming more and more reactionary as the crisis developed.

Later on, when I was unemployed myself and very much out of favour with the ecclesiastical authorities, I was in a much better position to argue the matter out with him, and we agreed that, even if he were right in his conclusions, no failure on the part of individuals or whole groups now living should be allowed to destroy our loyalty to Christ, to the Church and to posterity; that the validity of the Sacraments did not depend on the qualities of the ministers; and that public witness in the Church to our faith was a necessary part of our Christian obedience. There are fewer happier days in my recollection than the one in which, after long discussions, he began again a regular communicant life which continued to the day of his death.

Why then did G. L. and his friends go to prison? Shortly after the 1914-18 war a Labour Board of Guardians was called upon to administer an area in which, in its own words, ''the greater number of people always lived on the verge of starvation, plunged periodically into the deepest want of unemployment''; in which great numbers were living four and five to a room, and many six, seven or eight to a room. This in 1921. The Guardians had to face the growing problem of unemployment and destitution, and the impossibility of dealing with it under the conditions which confronted them. West London, with a rateable value of £15 millions, had 4,800 persons unemployed; East London, with a rateable value of £4 millions, had 86,500 unemployed. Thus, with only a quarter of the paying capacity of the West End, the East End had seventeen times the burden of unemployment to meet. The Guardians must either cut relief or raise the rates to astronomical heights. They refused to do either.

The Poor Law demanded that they should pay relief below that of the meanest wages in the district; that relief, in fact, should be governed by the standards that the most niggardly employer could enforce on his workmen. That, of course, acted as an incentive to work, and as a lever to keep wages down. If relief were raised above that level, none would work below it, and the level of wages would tend to rise. The Poor Law insisted that need must not be taken into account, and that the man with many children should not be paid above the general level. The Poplar Labour Group, actuated by simple Christian motives, insisted on relating relief to need, and demanded that in this impossible situation the richer boroughs—which, after all, were at least as responsible for the general situation as the poorer ones—should help to pay by an equalisation of the rates. It seemed to them to be a case of simple Christian justice, and for that cause they went to prison for six weeks. The auditor sent down to inspect the accounts could not find a single instance of fraud or dishonesty in their general administration, and was forced to fall back on one item of misuse of funds, namely, that, while they were in prison, £10 had been paid to a school band for playing outside the prison to cheer them up.

The charges against them were that they had defied the principle of the Poor Law of 1834, which said that "the amount of relief under the Poor Law should of necessity be calculated on a lower scale than the earnings of an independent labourer who maintains himself by his labour"; that they had inaugurated a new departure in Poor Law policy by "sending children of recipients of outdoor relief for a summer holiday at the expense of the rates"; that "the institution was regarded more as an alms-house than as a work-house". It was said that "too many newspapers and periodicals were given the inmates to read"; that "they had been given too many facilities for baths" and "too much water was being used''; and finally, ''that those too old or infirm or sick to work, were allowed out after breakfast all day and not forced to work or remain in the institution''. To these charges the thirty Guardians, with G. L. at their head, wrote *Guilty and Proud of It*, and went to prison for six weeks. They believed that ''the poor are poor because they are robbed, and robbed because they are poor'', a saying that might have come from St. Ambrose and many another Christian saint. They ''refused to treat poverty as a crime and paupers as criminals''.

Of course, they won their immediate fight and secured an equalisation of rates, and eventually a new method of administration, though that victory brought with it a whole set of new problems which had to be tackled stage by stage in the same spirit, and which, moreover, demanded the capture of the new centres of administration. But this vital concern for ''persons'' and common justice seemed to most of us characteristic of the Labour movement as a whole throughout the bitter struggles of the next twenty-five years, in spite of the difference of opinion on philosophy and tactics which at times seemed likely to tear it from its simple Christian moorings.

About that I want to say something later on. But it is significant to us that, when the last vestiges of the old Poor Laws have by Act of Parliament been abolished with a Labour Government in power, Aneurin Bevan, the Minister of Health, should instinctively talk of hotels and not institutions for the aged and infirm; should want to give them the money to pay their own bills so that they may not feel that they are paupers, or that poverty is a crime; that twenty-five years after the Poplar protest he should still, as the official spokesman of the party in power, be using the same language and be governed by the same set of values as G. L. was when he went to prison. It is something more perhaps than a happy coincidence that he should have so closely associated himself in this work with Charlie Key, who went to prison with Lansbury.

It was to such people that I came as a stranger to Poplar. At once I felt at home as I have never felt anywhere else. They were people who were thinking very much as I was thinking and who seemed to me to be actuated by the same set of values. Contact with them illuminated, made clear and brought together into a synthesis so much that I had learned about and experienced in Jesus. They were concerned about persons, and things only in so far as they helped to make personal life possible and personal relationships healthy.

In every party there are, of course, followers who accept a leadership without much thought, or who are caught up in a movement or an organisation without any real convictions. That is true of every political and social movement, as it is true of every section of the Church. Masses of people belong to this or that society without any real act of choice, but simply because they are brought up in it or somehow get caught up in it without any volition on their part. But the mainstream of the movement was obviously directed by Christian values and steeped in Christian ways of thought. It was led by people who had been genuinely converted to Socialism and whose lives bore witness to the fact that they were willing to make the sacrifices which their convictions demanded.

It is true that many of them had already ceased to go to church, but it seemed to me that what they called Socialism was very like the application of the values of Christ to the situation which confronted them. By fair means or foul the essential means of life had got into the hands of a few, and must be freed for the use of persons. So long as a few laid claim to an absolute ownership and control over those things, they had a life and death control over persons which was not only intolerable, but inhuman and unchristian. To them nationalisation was a means to end that domination, and no comparable alternative seemed to me to be offered elsewhere.

There seemed to me to be a whole set of Christian values

which fitted in with the outlook of the group as it fitted in with no other group of whom I had had experience. I do not mean to imply that these values were not to be found in individual members of other political parties, or to suggest for one moment that I first found Christians when I first found Socialists; but I did feel that at last I had found a group of people who helped me to gather together a lot of stray threads, and make a unity of thought and action where none existed before.

When people came to work with or for me now I did not ask them whether they were Tories or Socialists. But I did enquire in a much more realistic way as to the set of values by which they lived and acted. When we held them in common we could work together without constant friction, and they "belonged". Whatever their political allegiance, I could always count on the same sort of reactions to the same set of facts, and my job was to give them a living experience of those facts. The same unity of values led many who for some reason or other had become alienated from Christ and the Church towards a surrender to Him. If sometimes there was a refusal to face the cost of the implication of those values, that is in the nature of sinful human beings, including myself; but that fact did not invalidate this natural unity which seemed to me to exist.

Moreover, I found my eyes being opened to a new outlook on world affairs which fitted this unity. I used to sing "Land of hope and glory" . . . "God who made thee mighty make thee mightier yet", and "Britannia, rule the waves" with much gusto; now I found both distasteful. For though I could twist the words to mean something other than the writers and most singers of them meant, they represented something foreign to this life to which I now belonged, and to Christ who had not before opened my eyes to the sin of such Jingoism. Those who delighted to sing "Send him victorious, happy and glorious" or, even worse, who accepted the implications involved in "Scatter our enemies and make them fall; confound their politics, frustrate their knavish tricks'', meant something that I could no longer mean; and loved to place me in the dilemma of singing something distasteful, or appearing to be unpatriotic; and that I have never been.

At the University, when I regarded myself as non-political, I had debated against Home Rule for Ireland, and was a blatant Imperialist, because I just took Imperialism for granted, without questioning its relationship to my Christian beliefs. Now I found myself in favour of Home Rule on principle, speaking with Nehru in Trafalgar Square and joining the India Freedom League. I became a believer in a free Commonwealth of peoples, and regarded with dislike the symbols which emphasised the forcible subjection of one nation by another.

In fact, I found myself uncomfortable in many Christian circles where these values seemed either to be ignored or denied in practice, and more at home in circles where they were passionately held by people who may or may not have as yet seen their essential roots in Christ.

I suppose that, in common with most Christians, I had always believed that the Church had that particular duty to the poor and oppressed which runs as a thread throughout the Old and New Testaments; but here was a movement from the working class itself, rising out of the horrors of the Industrial Revolution, that seemed to embody much that Jesus taught, and to be expressing in one particular field, and that a very wide one, the principles which He laid down. Why should it be thought odd that the Christian Gospel should bear this fruit?

Whatever the sins of the Church, she cannot help but proclaim and uphold before the eyes of men the living Christ by whom alone they can be saved. If our sins sometimes blind men to the whole claims of Christ Jesus, nevertheless, in the measure in which He is witnessed to, there is fruit, and He draws men unto Himself. The life into which I came, though only too often divorced from the worshipping Church, was the result of the work of countless men and women who had laboured and taught, worshipped and maintained the means of grace, with much sacrifice, and died unknown and unsung.

God is always working in history; and it was not for nothing that He anticipated the Industrial Revolution by raising up Wesley, who in his little Bethels not only trained the leaders of a movement which was to grow among millions forcibly deprived of their birthright and condemned to the living hell of factory and mine and the slums of the new big cities, but also provided a faith by which it was not to grow godlessly. It was not for nothing that He raised up a great line of men like Kingsley and Maurice, Headlam and Conrad Noel, Scott Holland, Gore and Temple, who nourished that faith as the movement was growing to maturity.

Maurice Reckitt, in his book *From Maurice to Temple*, says that "A great opportunity for the Church of England offered itself for a moment in 1848. Three men perceived it and stood together as far as might be to seize it", and comments: "Who shall say what might have been the situation of the Church to-day if her response had been such that the effort could have been sustained?"[1] These men believed that the industrial system was a violation of natural law and that, in the words of Maurice, "God's order seems to me more than ever the antagonist of man's systems. Christian Socialism is to my mind the assertion of God's order".[2] They held that there was nothing for which this mass movement fought that was inconsistent with the teaching of the Church. But, if the Church as a whole did not follow their lead, there have always been some who have carried on that tradition. As a result the British working-class movement has always rejected quite decisively both the dogmatic materialism represented by such bodies as the Socialist Party of Great Britain[3]

[1] p. 68.

[2] Quoted in Reckitt, op. cit., p. 85.

[3] The Socialist Party of Great Britain is quite distinct from both the Labour Party and the Communist Party. It claims to preach pure Marxism and is dogmatically atheist. At one time it had a considerable following in London and elsewhere.

and its Continental allies, and the dialectic materialism of the Communist Party. Great though the influence of Karl Marx has been, and in many ways almost indispensable in helping them to understand the forces with which they were contending, and in introducing a dynamic force which continually lifted the movement out of the doldrums, the Labour movement has repeatedly rejected his philosophy as inconsistent with the beliefs it held as to the nature of persons. It has refused to comply with demands for actions which might cut the knot which tied the movement to its traditional Christian allegiance.

It is my firm conviction that as great an opportunity is offered the Church to-day as that which was offered in 1848. Are we again to fail to seize it?

Hammond says of the Church of that day that "the chief cause of the Church's unpopularity was . . . the feeling that the Church gave its sanction to all the injustices and abuses that degraded the poor and outraged their self-respect. . . . For the Church, like every other part of the system of aristocratic government, had been corrupted by the abuses that come thick and fast when the sense of property is stronger in any body of men than the sense of duty".[1] If that is not true of the Church in England to-day, it has been held to be true in our own time of the Church in Russia, in Spain and elsewhere on the Continent, with disastrous consequences. In so far as it is not true to-day of the Church in England, that fact is largely due to the stream of thought which Reckitt traces in his book *From Maurice to Temple*. But the test of the strength of the work of such men in the Church is yet to come. That chapter in our history is about to be opened.

Under the challenge of the second world war both the Church and the nation were forced to re-examine the foundations upon which our society rests. Malvern Conference, under the leadership of William Temple, spoke to the conscience of the Church. Its findings appeared in January 1941;

[1] *The Age of the Chartists*, p. 220. Quoted in Reckitt, op. cit., p. 22.

a month before that, the Archbishops of Canterbury and York, the Archbishop of Westminster and the Moderator of the Free Church Federal Council published a letter to *The Times* laying down a Christian basis upon which they were agreed.[1] An examination of these two documents leads me to the conclusion that the same forces which were active in the Church were active also in the minds of the people of our country when, at the end of the war, they deliberately put into power a Labour Government. Later on I want to examine this situation more closely, but it seems to me significant that at this crisis of our history the programme which the leaders of the Church agreed upon should have coincided so closely with that of this movement which grew out of the soil of poverty and misery through the strivings of the common people. Both are in essence attempts to relate eternal truth to the problems confronting men in their contemporary world. Both seek to maintain true foundations in that movement towards community which is the result of the Spirit of God working through the Church and through history.

The Church cannot, of course, as a Church, ally herself with any particular political party, for her message is to all men. Each person matters to her, not only in history, but beyond history. She stands in the world upholding before men the living Christ, who challenges the inadequacy of any human arrangement to express fully the values of His Kingdom. But it is the duty of the Church at all times to examine herself carefully as an institution, and her own earthly arrangements. She is bound to make certain that she is not, in fact, hindering the efforts of men to bring their lives into closer correspondence with the will of God, as a result of having become so deeply entangled in the structure of one social order that she is fearful of change; and, in particular, of change which will cost her members and herself, as an institution, much material prestige and sacrifice. She must, at all times, require her members to examine sympathetically

[1] 21st December 1940. See Appendix, p. 174.

any attempt by men of good will, whether within or without her worshipping life, towards the right ordering of society, believing that they correspond with the will of God even if they are not identified with it.

The faults which appear to be present in the British Labour movement are not inherent in the principles of the movement, but they are largely due to the unwillingness of Christians and others to take their share in its day-to-day work. But the large extent to which the movement has remained faithful to the Christian tradition, and the way in which it has consistently rejected every attempt on the part of some to tear it from that tradition, is due to the fact that there have always been many who were prepared to play their part in it at much sacrifice to themselves. It is because of this that, whatever the motive which actuates this or that member, the Labour movement is not in principle merely a selfish attempt to claim a share of liberty and material wealth, but is actually in principle, and can be made in fact, the political movement which in this England insists on the Christian doctrine of natural law, the value and significance of each person, and the acknowledgment of God as Creator of the material world for the use of men.

Within the Church itself there has been a steady stream of prophets seeking to interpret to the worshipping body this movement of the people towards community as the natural development of our democratic heritage, and in the direct line of the Christian tradition. There must be a determined effort now to link the whole together against the repudiation of that tradition, a repudiation which has led to the chaos of the modern world, and directly to two world wars.

It is my contention that the first steps towards the coming together of these two streams occasioned the coming into power of the Labour Government in 1945. An examination of the situation between the two wars and of the events which led up to that result I must leave to a later chapter. Upon the success or failure of that Government the immediate future not only of our own country but of Europe seems to depend; for I can see no possible alternative for those who, like myself, believe that God has through the history of the last century called us to this adventure.

If this common movement towards community fails, the consequences for this nation and for the world will be disastrous and will inevitably lead to a fight between dictatorships of the right and of the left. In that event Christ will continue through His Body, the Church, to offer to man the means and the hope of salvation. That is our faith. But the cost to Him and to mankind through the failure of the members of His visible body in this generation to respond to the demands which He now makes on us will be great indeed.

Many things have happened since those early days in Poplar. Chronic unemployment, revolution and war have tested the faith of millions. The challenge to Christianity and to Social Democracy becomes daily more insistent. We cannot meet it by wishful thinking or by drawing up fanciful paper schemes on "if only" lines.

It is my hope that the story of my experiences during the inter-war years may help some to a clearer understanding of the present situation; to a truer assessment of the various forces at work in it; and to a readier obedience to the call of God to them at this moment.

3

THE PEOPLE OF THE EAST END BETWEEN THE WARS

IT is not easy to think back accurately to those years after the first world war and to see ourselves as we were then. On the whole, my recollection of the Poplar of those days is of a general optimism as to the future, in spite of the fact that there was much poverty and suffering and that unemployment was steadily rising. My experiences in the trenches had proved to me that men will endure almost anything provided that they feel that they are engaged on a task which is worth while and that they do not despair of the future. The thing which first struck my notice in Poplar was this feeling of a people looking forward with hope. That hope was not occasioned by any act of the then Government: on the contrary, there was no surer way of raising a laugh at a meeting than by reading a speech of Lloyd George's about "Homes fit for heroes to live in" or similar rhetoric. Somehow a leadership had arisen from among the workers themselves which made them feel that they were not helpless nonentities, but that they were engaged in a crusade for a different sort of life, in which they would have a decisive voice in the way their lives were to be lived. In spite of their hunger and bad housing they were alive, interested in what was going on, and looking ahead with confidence.

They were reading, and reading good books at that. The Library at Poplar was always crowded with people, and I remember how eager the staff there were to see that the newest and best books were available for them. The churches still had good congregations, and a good mixture of dockers, railwaymen and manual workers of all kinds. At St. Michael's we were running several study circles every week, with a large Bible-class for men on Sundays. At nights there were regular open-air meetings in the streets where we talked and argued about religion and politics and economics indiscriminately.

I remember so well both the seriousness and the fun of those meetings—serious because we knew that the things we were talking about were matters of life and death. Neither parson nor politician could get away with claptrap before that crowd of eager intelligent people. We parsons had to be careful what we said, because some of them would come into church on the Sunday, and at the next open-air meeting criticise anything we did in church which was to their minds inconsistent with what we said outside. And there was fun, too, because we were what we called ourselves, comrades, and the give and take of those meetings, though often hard hitting, was between friends.

And again, so many were eager to try their hand at speaking or even writing. Men like Johnny Cox, who, when he was not travelling round the world, was arguing or writing pamphlets. I have one of his still which drew a post card from Bernard Shaw on which was written: "Is your paper any good? Good! ! ! What for? ? ?" We knew Johnny too well to let him get on to a platform, for once there, nobody could get him off. He got his chance one night when the Chairman of an I.L.P. meeting did not turn up, to offer himself and to be accepted in his place by those who did not know him. They took an hour to get him off and stop his flow of words, and then only by force, much to our amusement. "I won't be interrupted; I'm Chairman of this meeting" was his reply to every attempt to stem his eloquence.

There were packed meetings in the Town Hall on every conceivable subject, crowded Labour Party ward meetings and branch meetings of the unions; regular processions to Trafalgar Square, not only to call attention to this or that matter which we felt deeply, but sometimes because we felt that we must do such things together in order to express that which we held in common. Gayer and gayer they became, with banners flying, and carts and horses bedecked; with organised shows and tableaux on wheels; and children in their best, gay with maypole and dance. Always we were welcomed there as Christians, headed by the crucifix and carrying other Christian symbols. Now and again there was a hint of what was to come as we clashed with the police on the question of the route to be taken and our dislocation of the traffic in the West End; for we were in those days in no mood to fit ourselves into either the Sunday or the back-street peace. May Day was May Day, convenient or inconvenient to ourselves or to others.

The people felt that a future lay before them in which they had a vital part to play. They had captured several Borough Councils, and looked forward to capturing the London County Council and beyond that Parliament. The victory which the Poplar Guardians had won in prison helped in the process of shifting much power over local affairs from the local centre to a much less responsible and intimate one in County Hall and Westminster—a process which went on steadily as the years went by. In some ways we recognised that this was a good thing, and in any case inevitable; but it was an early warning of much that was to follow. An impotent feeling came as we found ourselves caught up in a machine administered by people whom we did not know, who seemed to be directly responsible to no one, and who did not seem to care. It was, therefore, important that we should go forward to capture those centres of power in public life.

It was not long before we became aware that so far we had but taken part in skirmishes in a battle which was taking place on a much wider field, and that a grim time lay ahead. It soon became obvious that a great attempt was being made all over the world by a close-knit organisation of big business to break the growing power of the working class. The international unity of that group was clearly demonstrated by the attempt on an international scale to break Russia. The reaction of the working class to this is well worth study, and helps much to an understanding of their attitude to-day. The Communists were but a tiny fraction in the East End and had little following; but in general there was a fierce resentment against this attempt to destroy by international force and boycott a people who, men felt, had been forced to rebel against an unbearable tyranny, and who were trying desperately to establish some sort of order out of the chaos that resulted.

They felt that if there were no other way to freedom than by a violent revolution, the people were right to take it. They believed that the Russians had taken the only course open to them. If that was to be met by a common onslaught of the other capitalist powers, they felt instinctively that, however remote Communist theory and practice was from their own, Russia was bearing the first onslaught of the attack which would naturally and inevitably follow on the workers elsewhere if Russia were beaten. The fact, too, that the Church in Russia seemed to be so closely interwoven with the old Czarist régime, and that those who were attempting to destroy the new Republic were in close communication not only with the White Russians, but with certain leaders of that Church, gave point to the oft-repeated Communist slogan that "religion is the opium of the people" and "the greatest tool in the hands of the ruling class to keep the people under". It made the workers more ready to pay attention to Marxist propaganda.

I shall never forget the little Russian barber who told Jack Bucknall and me one day, when we asked him what the Church taught in Russia before the revolution, "The Great Father—the Little Father; God—the Czar; they made them one." That remark was paralleled shortly after by a man resplendent in uniform on the steps of one of the Government offices in Whitehall—I think it was the War Office—on a day when the King was going to open Parliament. In a reply to a question of mine, "Can you tell me what time the King comes by?" I was quite taken aback to hear from such a quarter, "I don't know. I'm an atheist".

With this international solidarity of the real rulers of the big powers with the White Russians, and their financing of the expeditions of Deniken, Koltchak, Wrangel and Yudenich one after the other, was coupled their boycott of the attempts of the Social Democrats to achieve some sort of economic order out of the chaos in post-war Germany (a boycott which broke the ground and prepared it for the later sowing of Hitler and the harvest of the second world war), and the welcome given by the ruling classes to the rise to power of Mussolini. These things together did much to convince the British working class of the reality of a class struggle of bigger dimensions than anything they had before envisaged. They were now convinced that their turn was coming and that a major attempt would soon be made not only to reduce the British workers' standard of life, but to break their rising power and solidarity.

At home the process of the rationalisation of industry was beginning to increase the sufferings of the workers. It resulted in the increase of unemployment by the displacement of many "hands" as the gap widened between what the workers produced and their purchasing power. Together with the lengthening of the unemployment queues came the preparations for a major attack on their standard of life. The first target of that attack was to be, as so often before, the miners.

If Keynes had warned the country of the danger and futility of the Government's foreign policy, the Government's own Sankey Commission had pointed to the only possible way of dealing with the chaos in the coal industry. A majority of the Sankey Commission, including the Chairman, reported in favour of nationalisation, and the Government refused to carry out their recommendations in spite of the Prime Minister's pledge to Bob Smillie that they would do so. The pledge was as follows:

11 DOWNING STREET,
WHITEHALL, S.W.
21st March 1919.

DEAR SIR,

Speaking in the House of Commons last night I made a statement in regard to the Government's policy in connection with the report of the Coal Industry Commission.

I have pleasure in confirming, as I understand you wish me to do, my statement that the Government are prepared to carry out in the spirit and in the letter the recommendation of Sir John Sankey's Report.

Yours faithfully,
A. BONAR LAW.[1]

But the Government went back on their promise, and proposed instead a vague scheme which no one took seriously and which was soon forgotten.

In 1924 the Labour Party made the fatal error of accepting office with a majority in the House against them. Mr. Asquith called it a Labour Government "with its claws cut", and added: "The experiment could hardly be made under safer conditions . . . we still sleep more or less comfortably in our beds. Capital steadily pursues its old routine of continuous, and, on the whole, prosperous investment."[2] Under such conditions the Labour Government could do little. Though it did manage to restore the legal minimum wage in agriculture, raise the old age pensions scale, and, most important of all, pass the Wheatley Housing Act, which was the first real attempt to provide houses for letting at working-class rents, and under which eventually 520,000 houses were built in England and Wales, it came to an ignominious end with the Zinoviev letter scandal.

As soon as the Tories were back in power preparations

[1] Quoted in Allen Hutt, *Post-War History of the British Working Class*, p. 19.

[2] Speech to the National Liberal Federation. Quoted in Hutt, op. cit., p. 77 f.

were resumed for the attack on the miners; and in June 1925 the coal-owners gave notice to terminate the existing agreement and proposed drastic wage cuts. This move obviously had Government backing, for a month later Mr. Baldwin, the Prime Minister, stated quite plainly to the miners' representatives that the Government were prepared to back the coal-owners, and themselves regarded this attempt to lower the miners' wages as a prelude to an attack on the standard of life of the whole working class.

"*Miners:* But what you propose means a reduction of wages.

"*Prime Minister:* Yes. All the workers in this country have got to face a reduction of wages.

"*Miners:* What do you mean?

"*Prime Minister:* I mean all the workers of this country have got to take reductions in wages to help put industry on its feet."

(*Daily Herald*, 31/7/25.)

This clear declaration by the Prime Minister at the outset of the dispute makes nonsense of the Government's later pretensions that it acted throughout impartially. All this was, of course, bound up with the restoration of the Gold Standard in April 1925. Mr. Keynes, writing immediately after this return to gold, says: "Mr. Churchill's policy of improving the exchange by 10 per cent was, sooner or later, a policy of reducing everyone's wages by 2s. in the £. He who wills the end wills the means. What now faces the Government is the ticklish task of carrying out their own dangerous and unnecessary decision."[1]

On the history of the preparations on both sides for the inevitable struggle which was to follow, I need not dwell; it has been told over and over again. In these preparations on the Government side and during the strike itself the Marxian thesis that in a capitalist society the real governing power

[1] "The Economic Consequences of Mr. Churchill", 1925. Keynes's *Essays in Persuasion*, p. 245.

in a country is the group who own and control the means of production, and that the State is but the instrument by which they maintain their power, was made to seem a not inapt description of the real state of affairs.

The half-hearted efforts on the part of the leaders of the workers to prepare for the struggle, and the way in which they were afterwards accused of "grovelling for peace", was due to the fact that they never had any revolutionary intent. They were determined to stand true to the original issues at stake—justice and a decent standard of life for the miners—and not to allow the struggle to degenerate in any way into a fight on constitutional issues. "I suppose my usual critics will say that Thomas was almost grovelling, and it is true," said Mr. Thomas. "In all my long experience . . . I never begged and pleaded like I begged and pleaded all day to-day, and I pleaded not alone because I believed in the case of the miners, but because in my bones I believed that my duty to my country involved it."[1]

On the other side the whole of big business came together, built up their volunteer strike-breaking organisation, the O.M.S., with the active support of the Government, who welcomed it as an auxiliary to their own plans, and told the public that they would be "performing a patriotic act" by joining it.

In spite of this the workers' leaders continued negotiations, and an agreement was reached which only required the endorsement of the miners' leaders, when the Government acted. The printers of the *Daily Mail* refused to print an article which in their opinion prejudiced the issues at stake. Headed "For King and Country", it declared that the General Strike was "a revolutionary movement, intended to inflict suffering on the great mass of innocent people in the community . . . it must be dealt with by every resource at the disposal of the community".[2] The Govern-

[1] Hutt, op. cit., p. 130.

[2] Hutt, op. cit., p. 133 f. Or see Cole and Postgate, *The Common People*, ch. 44, for the history of the General Strike.

ment used this refusal by a group of workers to print an article which would inflame the public against the whole case of the trade unions as a pretext to call off all negotiations. The T.U.C. immediately sent a deputation to inform the Prime Minister that they repudiated the unofficial action of the *Daily Mail* machine men. They found 10 Downing Street in darkness. A servant informed them that the Prime Minister had gone to bed, and that their further presence was undesirable.

A careful reading of all the negotiations at that time seems to me to lead only to one conclusion. It is that a decision had been reached by the Cabinet that the time had come to teach the workers a lesson. In December 1925 Mr. Churchill had stated: "We decided to postpone the crisis in the hope of averting it, or if not of averting it, of coping effectually with it when the time came."[1] The Cabinet had agreed with workers' leaders to issue a statement two days before the strike, declaring that "The Prime Minister has satisfied himself, as a result of the conversations he has had with the representatives of the Trades Union Congress, that, if negotiations are continued (it being understood that the notices[2] cease to operate), the representatives of the Trades Union Congress are confident that a settlement can be reached on the lines of the report within a fortnight".[3] In view of that it is difficult to avoid the conclusion that the Government welcomed the opportunity given to it by the action of a handful of workers on the *Daily Mail* to break the power of the trade-union movement as a prelude to a general attack on the standard of life of the whole of the working class.

I feel equally sure that the mass of the workers had no revolutionary intent. Their general attitude during the strike was in keeping with that, although they were constantly

[1] Speech in House of Commons on 10th December 1925. *Hansard*, col. 733.

[2] i.e. lock-out notices.

[3] Prime Minister in the House of Commons, 5th May 1926. *Hansard*, col. 411.

being provoked to take a more militant attitude. It is true that, at the back of their minds, they realised that the Government's policy was an attack on them all; but the resistance they put up, and the solidarity of their ranks, arose mainly because they just could not stand by and see the miners defeated alone. They wished merely to register a solid "No" to a premeditated attack on their mates, and, through them, on the whole of the working classes.

The spontaneity and solidarity of their response to the call, when it came, was amazing. I well remember meeting an old docker, Alf Middleton, who was a regular communicant at St. Michael's, that first evening, and hearing him remark: "John, I've been in every dock strike since I was a boy, and this is the first time there was no need for pickets. They're all out, from the pay-office clerks downwards."

But, in spite of the fact that on the workers' side there was no thought of an attack on the constitution, the Government not only did its best through its news sheets and the B.B.C. to convince the general public that they were out to emulate the Bolsheviks, but did all it could to provoke them to acts which would give colour to this pretence.

My own personal experience was, of course, confined to London, and more immediately to the East End. There, we were continuously engaged in trying to keep the original issues to the fore, and to prevent open breaches of the peace, against repeated acts of provocation on the part of the authorities. There were, of course, certain incidents: some of them by a few irresponsibles; some by children and the usual East End toughs; some in anger at direct acts of provocation. I remember one day, when a big crowd was milling in quite good temper round the dock gates near Blackwall Tunnel with a large force of mounted police in attendance, I saw a young boy about ten years old pick up a horseshoe which was lying in the road, and toss it into that crowd of mounted police. Immediately truncheons were out and a great many men took a severe beating-up.

Incidents like this are almost unavoidable in such tense situations, and, of course, they provide opportunities for those who are looking for trouble on either side; nor is it fair to blame the police if they are provoked to take action when the situation seems to be getting beyond their control. But such situations were not all indicative of the general temper during the early days of the strike. The mass of the people did their best to keep calm and to avoid clashes. On the whole we were successful, because of the tactics we pursued. When the Specials came, looking very uncomfortable in their rig-out, we just stood in a semicircle and stared at them. They generally kept near a telephone booth, into which they retreated. We dispersed as they phoned for assistance. Their existence in our midst was a provocation in itself, for, on the whole, they represented a "class" intrusion from the public schools; but our tactic was to make fun of them rather than allow angry words and abuse to lead to violence.

On the other hand, the tactics pursued from the other side seemed to us to be directed towards provoking violence. In spite of the fact that we offered to cart the necessary food from the docks, the country was told that we were trying to starve the nation; and not only was our offer refused, but convoys guarded by armoured vehicles and machine-guns were sent to fetch it out. That might have caused a nasty situation had we not joked it off by our slogan, "Let them fetch out the food and we will eat it". When they provoked us further by lining the streets with soldiers, bayonets and all, we replied by the slogan, "Each girl take a soldier", knowing that such fraternisation was the best way to avoid conflict.

Every night that trouble seemed likely because of the crowd of sightseers out in the streets those of us who could speak and were known got on chairs and persuaded the crowd to disperse. We were helped in that by the local Chief Inspector—a decent fellow, who knew us and did not want trouble; and who, on at least two occasions to my knowledge, and at my request, held his police off to give us time to do the job ourselves.

On the whole we succeeded in avoiding any serious clash till that last day, after the strike had been called off; and that, I believe, was engineered from outside. I have never been able to understand why that attack was made on a perfectly peaceful crowd waiting in front of the Town Hall for news of the settlement, unless someone had deliberately prepared it. News had come through on the wireless that the strike was over. But, quite naturally, men were not prepared to go back to work until they had received official information; and there was a general movement to the Poplar Town Hall to await the news of the terms of settlement. The crowd grew so thick in Newby Place, not only with men, but with the wives and children they had brought with them, that the Mayor opened the Town Hall and put as many of the women and children as possible in there, where they entertained themselves with a singsong.

In the meantime several of us were helping to beguile the time by speaking to the crowd outside. They were in good humour and were laughing and joking among themselves. I had just finished speaking when suddenly a big van came round the corner from the direction of the High Street and charged straight for the crowd. There were shouts and curses as it crashed through at great speed. Several people were hurt, but amazingly no one was killed. It was going too fast to stop till it reached East India Dock Road, where it drew up and disgorged a squad of police with their batons drawn. As they advanced down the street in line towards the crowd it was obvious not only that they meant business, but that there was no time for the crowd to disperse. I managed to get through the crowd and reach the police while they were still some twenty or thirty yards away. I was all alone and in my cassock; the Inspector in charge was new to me and behind the line of police. I asked him if he could tell me what was wrong, but received no answer. I then said that the crowd was waiting for orders and suggested that, if he wanted them to disperse, he should give them time to do so. All this time I was being steadily pushed backwards. Then suddenly I was floored by a rain of batons which left me half senseless on the ground with a broken finger and bruises on my head and shoulders. Then they rushed the crowd, beat many of them up mercilessly, stormed into the Town Hall and into the Mayor's Parlour and dispersed with so much violence those sitting there that the Mayor's arm was broken and much of his furniture smashed.

When I recovered I made my way to the police station to protest, and found there a number of men who had been arrested. My protest being of no avail—for the Chief Inspector was as ignorant as I was as to the reason for these happenings—I made my way to Sam March, our local Member of Parliament, and later to the hospital to have my injuries attended to. While I was there I heard that a minority, in retaliation for all this, were concocting a plan to burn down the police station, and made my way to their meeting-place. I learned that the rumour had got about that I had been killed. By showing myself alive, and by argument, some of us persuaded them to give up the idea of retaliation. The fact that we were able to do so without much trouble is evidence not only of our hatred of violence, but of the discipline in our ranks even when tempers were high. Some say still that we were wrong in this; but I believe that any sort of retaliation would have given those responsible for the outrage the justification they were seeking, and that a reign of terror would have resulted.

It was after midnight when I got home, to find a crowd in my house; and not till I got rid of them did I go to bed. I was awakened about 3 a.m. by a banging at the door, and looked out to see four men at the door and a car standing at the kerb. On my enquiring what they wanted, I was informed that I was wanted at Scotland Yard at once, and that they had been sent to fetch me. I asked whether they had a warrant for my arrest, and on hearing that they had none, I refused to admit them into the house. In the morning I rang up Scotland Yard and asked whether it was true that they wanted me; and told my story to them. Within the hour they sent officers down to enquire, and to deny knowledge of the incident. A policeman was stationed outside my house for days afterwards.

Some people thought at the time that the whole thing was an attempt by the police in plain clothes to prevent me from giving evidence at the Thames Police Court the next day. I feel fairly certain, however, from the attitude of the men, that it was the work of a few members of the already growing Union of Fascists, who naturally in this situation had joined forces with "big business" against the trade unions, as they did all over the world, and wanted to "take me for a ride".

The next day Sam March and I went to the Thames Police Court to give evidence at the prosecution of those who had been arrested. The magistrate, Mr. Cairns, one of the fairest we have ever had in the East End, was obviously nonplussed by the whole affair. He listened carefully to the various accounts, and then asked me whether I could produce any evidence to support my story. I told him that I could bring hundreds; for not only were the women in the Town Hall, with windows overlooking the square, objective witnesses, but there were many others in the grounds and on the steps of the parish church who saw the whole affair. It was from their letters of sympathy that I pieced together some of the incidents later on. Mr. Cairns dismissed all the summonses, and the arrested men came away with us.

The Poplar Borough Council tried for months afterwards to get the Home Secretary, Mr. Joynson Hicks, to hold an enquiry into the incident; and the whole story is recorded in the Minutes of that Council. The last I heard was that the Home Secretary said that: "If any individual who was injured could identify the individual policeman who had injured him, he would allow a prosecution." He refused to see a deputation of the Poplar Borough Council, stating in the House of Commons: "Any specific statement by persons who feel themselves aggrieved by the action of the police will also receive full investigation."[1]

Now, I do not altogether blame the police for what happened. The Prime Minister, Stanley Baldwin, had, in my opinion, already anticipated such a situation by the various statements he made in which he promised to support "blacklegs" and others who assisted in breaking the strike. In particular, on 8th May a proclamation was made in the *British Gazette* which stated "all ranks of the Armed Forces of the Crown are hereby notified that any action which they may find it necessary to take in an honest endeavour to aid the Civil Power will receive both now and afterwards the full support of His Majesty's Government".[2]

The police, after all, are the instruments of the Government in power, and act under orders. It is necessary, too, to bear in mind that in 1919, a few years before the General Strike, the police themselves had struck,[3] and a drastic purge had taken place in their ranks of those likely to act sympathetically with the working class in a crisis. Many of those who had been turned out, and whom we called "Lansbury's Lambs", were with us for many years after, and we learned from them much of value as to the habits and methods within the police force now that they were able to speak freely. Rarely do they engineer situations without at least knowing that what they do will escape censure and is in general line with the policy of the powers that be. I know personally a great many of them who hate being forced into such situations.

There seemed to be general agreement that these men guilty of violence had been drafted into Poplar for this particular job, and that they had been well primed beforehand; certainly they were not of our division, and the Inspector in charge was not the one with whom we had had such friendly

[1] *Hansard*, col. 2444, 17th June 1926. (See also *Hansard*, col. 1671, 10th June 1926.)

[2] See *Hansard*, cols. 765-6, 785-6, 10th May 1926. Also Hutt, op. cit., p. 137.

[3] Cole, *Condition of Britain*, pp. 429-34.

dealings during the strike itself. Some of the police later told me, by way of excuse, that they had been filled with all sorts of tales of rioting in Poplar, and that, since some boys had stoned their van earlier in the day, they cruised about looking for a crowd on whom they could get their own back. But, once the attack had begun, the police lost their heads and careered round Poplar beating up people half a mile away from the Town Hall. That night after the strike was certainly worse than any night during the strike itself. It seemed that the authorities were determined to push home their "lesson".

Now, the General Strike marks a decisive point not only in the history of the British working class, but in world history. The breaking of the power of the trade-union movement in Britain enabled the Government to continue quite ruthlessly, and without opposition, a policy which led inevitably to the slump of the 'thirties, the growth of Fascism and the second world war.

Among the working class the first reaction was a swing to the left and a looking to Communist leadership. Before the end of the year membership of the Communist Party doubled. Though a great many who joined slowly dribbled out again, the influence of the Communist Party in the movement generally, particularly through the "Minority Movement" and the "Left Wing Movement", remained. As a result the Labour Party for a time slumped badly; but later there was a turning to political action, which resulted in the putting into office of MacDonald's Government in 1929 (again with a majority in the House against them). But the Labour Party had learned no lesson from the 1924 débâcle. It was afraid to introduce any drastic measure to deal with the situation, and dithered about until the Party split into fragments and made way for the Coalition Government in 1931, and the long political wilderness.

The real struggle in such a situation was going on, of course, in the industrial field. On the one hand, the impact of the world depression led to reduction of the wages of those remaining in work, while unemployment increased to about 3¾ million at its peak in 1932. As the purchasing power of the masses fell, the slump became worse. On the other hand, resistance was continued by certain sections within the trade-union movement, including the unemployed themselves, who were organised principally by the National Unemployed Workers' Movement and led by such stalwart fighters as Wal Hannington and Ellen Wilkinson.

But though the numbers of the Communist Party remained small, there was a decided turn towards Marx, both as a guide to action and as offering a working philosophy of life, which affected greatly the character of the working class in general for many years to come. For the first time I became conscious of a widespread resentment against the Church, because she seemed neither to be attempting to understand the situation the working class were in, nor to be capable of rendering any visible help to them in their struggle. It was heartrending to people like me to witness not only their physical sufferings, but their gradual acquiescence in a philosophy of life which was alien to their tradition.

I suppose that it is impossible for anyone who was not in close contact with workers in industrial areas to understand their sufferings during this period. I often wish that those who grumble at small deprivations now would go back and remember those days and the physical and spiritual effects on millions.

While we were trying, of course, to do all we could to better material conditions, the fights round them involved much more fundamental ones. There could be no radical change in the situation of the workers unless faith in their own natural organisations and associations was restored, and a sense of their own dignity and personal worth maintained, in the face of forces which tended to destroy both.

Our local position did not differ much from that of our comrades elsewhere. It was not only that millions were unemployed and living below starvation level, but that millions of others were holding on to their jobs by the skin of their teeth, and at the cost of a loss of self-respect which wellnigh broke their hearts. Had we in London wished to shut our eyes to the sufferings of our comrades all over Britain, we would not have been allowed to do so; for the lines of hunger marchers converged on London from Scotland, Jarrow, Durham and South Wales. Miners were singing in our streets, begging for bread. Young girls were pouring into the metropolis looking for work, driven from their homes by the dreaded Means Test, only to be caught up, many of them, into prostitution and other forms of slavery. In Stepney, where I was during this period, the Church had to open a special hostel to house them and care for their babies until we could again either restore them to their homes or find work for them; and we were always full to capacity. To these were added the young lads, for whom the Fellowship of St. Christopher opened home after home. It is good to remember that there were many in the Church ready to help, even if the vast majority of Christians remained apathetic and left the main burden to others.

The unemployed themselves kept alive the spirit of unity, and for those who were sympathetic there were special opportunities for expressing their solidarity with them in their struggle. I could not count the number of times we marched to and from Hyde Park in the company of the hunger marchers, and tried to tell the public something of what all this suffering meant. We organised concerts to cheer those who were housed in the work-house in Poplar because there was nowhere else for them to go. In those early days at Christ Church, Watney Street, the congregation collected food and coal to give a northern contingent warmth and a hot meal on their arrival. When we had everything ready we found that they had been directed to a neighbouring school and locked in; and we had to cart all our stuff in cans about half a mile, climb up and put our food, now nearly cold, through the windows to those hungry men. How glad they were of that meal, and more, perhaps, of that gesture of friendship!

Coal! How much then and now hung on coal? Compare the method of dealing with it now with those years. Whatever mistakes that gallant friend Arthur Cook made, he loved his men and killed himself trying to avert that slow starvation and misery! I am proud to have stood beside him on many platforms.

Somehow, below the cracks in our unity which were visible in the upper structure of our movement, there was a real comradeship which persisted in spite of the seeming apathy, and which showed itself in action from time to time on both the national and international front as the presage of better things to come. It came to the surface in the attempt to help those marchers; in demonstrations for the freedom of India; in the way in which we tried to give help to the workers in Spain; in the collections for the Basque children; and in the growing resistance to the Fascists openly organising under Mosley.

Whatever his personal feelings, the East Ender was not going to allow an outsider to exploit our internal difficulties for political advantage. The day when the matter came to a head, and Mosley announced his intention to march with his Blackshirts through the East End, will not readily be forgotten. Clashes there had been before, but it was so obvious that this insult was to be resisted, with blood if necessary, that some of us went to Whitehall on a deputation, to let the authorities know exactly what that feeling was. They told us that they must allow the march to go on; and we told them in turn that no force could get Mosley through. On that morning, with no real leadership, but with an almost unanimous spontaneity, the East End swarmed to its western approaches and blocked them thousands deep. There was no force capable of shifting those crowds; and in reserve the paving-stones were torn up behind, and barricades erected, with carts and barrels and anything which lay to hand.

Whatever anybody else thought, it was to many of us a sign and a portent. It was a sign that, in spite of all that apathy and seeming indifference caused by years of suffering, there were some things which could bring to life a unity and a determination that augured well for the future. No people could be finally beaten down to slavery who were capable of exhibiting spontaneously such a unity in a matter on which they seemed outwardly to be hopelessly divided. When it came to the pinch they dropped their differences and united against a common enemy. It was a portent proving that things could be driven too far; that, beyond a point, men would not budge; that tyranny would be resisted; and that revolution, even to the point of bloodshed, was not the impossibility in England that many reckoned on, but that, while the workers would groan under the whip, and grin and bear it, they would revolt under the scorpion. The whips were there sure enough. Numbers of our able-bodied men were unemployed for many years, after twenty years of steady work. Their wives were doing a little scrubbing in the City; their younger children were working—they were cheap labour.

Perhaps it was not so bad while they were on statutory benefit, and drew their money as a right, though that was bad enough. It meant much, no doubt, to be treated still as persons with rights to benefit, but the scale even then for a man and wife and three children on full standard benefit was only 29s. 3d. a week. Once they came, however, on that dreaded means test, they knew what it meant in human suffering to lose that status.

Somebody once said to me: "But isn't it right that the household income should be pooled, and that the children should help their parents when their parents are unemployed?" I tried to tell him what thousands went through not for months, but for years. I tried to get him to see what it must feel like for an able-bodied father to be almost entirely dependent on his children for food and rent; and completely dependent for things like baccy and beer if such things were possible; what it feels like for a father and mother to have to go to their children between the ages of fourteen and eighteen for money, and to know that the pittance they were receiving on relief was reduced with each petty rise in the children's earnings.

Here are some extracts from a report drawn up by an official committee of the Church in Stepney at the time, after examining budgets of unemployed families: "The average of those budgets has been taken, and, after deductions have been made for rent, light and fuel, we arrive at the absurd sum of 2s. 7d. per head per week as the average amount for food of an unemployed person's family. In no budget is there any provision made for boots and clothes." Again, the same document, commenting on the effects on family life, says: "After a prolonged period of unemployment, many men are sent to the residential training centres at Belmont, Hollesley Bay or Dunton Farm. In such cases the choice is ultimately between accepting the Committee's order and going to gaol. The point we wish to raise is not the adequacy of the training, which is a matter of grave doubt, nor even the amount of brushes, mats, desks, chairs and tables, etc., which the London County Council has provided for it by this forced labour, but rather the attitude of mind which treats the unemployed person as a criminal and uses Belmont and such places as a threat." Later, in a comment on family life, the report continues: "The operation of the Means Test renders saving impossible on the part of children who are working if members of their families are unemployed. As an example, we quote a case from a parish in this Deanery where a widower is refused relief because he cannot attend a non-residential training school, and three children who are at work keep the whole family of six on the 25s. weekly they earn between them. The tragedy in the lives of those young wage-earners, for whom marriage is impossible, is less noticeable in their complaints than in its spiritual and moral results. In general, whether they stay at home and keep their parents, or whether they leave home altogether, the net result is the breaking-up of family life as we Christians desire to have it."

And here is a copy of an application for relief by one of our regular communicants at Christ Church, much better off financially because four of his children were working:

Applicant: Man claiming benefit for himself, wife and three dependent children aged 12, 11 and 7 years.
Occupation: Boiler scaler.
Other members of the family:

	£	s.	d.
A. Son aged 24. Boiler scaler, unemployed, Standard U.B.		15	3
B. Son aged 25. Unemployed, refused transitional benefit		—	
C. Daughter aged 23. Tobacco packer. Gross wages	2	5	0
D. Daughter aged 18. Tobacco worker. Gross wages	1	6	2
E. Son aged 14. Wages		12	0
Applicant allowed each week		10	0
Total income of family ..	5	8	5
Rent, insurance, etc. ..	1	5	4
	£4	3	1

Leaving a family of ten persons, four of them working, to live on 8s. 3d. a week per head.

Here, too, is an extract from an article of mine in the *Daily Herald* of 20th March 1934: "Come farther down the street: a girl of eighteen, a seamstress on piecework. Working hard for long hours, she can earn 25s. to 30s. a week. There is a father, mother, and brother of fifteen at school to be kept. On transitional benefit the father is allowed 10s. a week. That girl has to throw in all her money to keep the family. The father is only about fifty, so the girl not only has no life of her own now, but sees life through those spectacles years ahead."

How hard we tried by processions, speeches, articles and

agitations to make the public see what was happening to persons in this land ten to fifteen years after the end of the first world war! Let me quote from a sermon I preached in St. Paul's Cathedral in 1934: "I wonder if you who live outside our derelict areas have any idea of what it means to live under the conditions forced upon so many of our people, what it is like never to know any privacy, never to have undressed in a room without others of both sexes being there, never to have slept by yourself, never to have been alone. I wonder if you know what it is like to be unemployed for a long time, and see no hope of working again.

"I have lived in the East End for twelve years, and I have never seen such depression as exists to-day, and I would to God that we, who live amongst it, could make the world realise the effects of it upon our people. Not merely physical effects—those are bad enough—but the spiritual and mental effects. Can you imagine for yourself what it is like to be unemployed, not for a week or a month, but for years, until you begin to feel that you will never be in regular work again? And that amongst people in like condition as yourself, whole streets of them; and even those in work with no sense of security, never knowing when their turn will come. Bit by bit your home goes into the melting-pot, as articles are pawned in trying to meet the need. Visited regularly by the Relieving Officer, who has to pry into all your resources and dictate to you about the cleaning of your home and the way you keep your children, every available resource under the Means Test is taken into account so that your children's earnings are taken to keep you and the rise in their wages taken off your relief. Where no neighbour or relation is allowed to help you, since the amount of their help is deducted from your allowance; where, if a son living away from home tries to give his parents extra nourishment, that amount is deducted too and his payment made legal—so neighbourliness is destroyed in the interests of economy; where after a time you are forced away to a colony like Belmont, and kept there on and off for years;

where refusal to submit to the orders of the machine means prosecution for neglect of your children—a choice between submission and prison.''

In the article written for the *Daily Herald* from which I have already quoted I continued: ''I hate giving particular instances, because they are likely to be taken as isolated; but here is a normal one from my own parish, of an old woman who died last year. She was receiving relief, but her son who was living the other side of London—a labourer—offered to give her two shillings a week to provide extra nourishment that he felt she needed. Honest old woman that she was, she told the Relieving Officer. The payment was made legal, and the two shillings were deducted from her allowance by the Public Assistance Committee. But the inquisition goes farther. A close watch is kept on the house by the authorities: it must be kept clean, and the inhabitants constantly questioned, lest by any chance they might be picking up a bob or so that can be deducted from relief. In fact, 'home' becomes no longer a private, but a public, affair.''

As for the charge of prosecution for the neglect of children: I wonder how many people to-day realise that where a family refused to comply with the demand to refuse food to one member of it who was ordered to Belmont, a ''cat and mouse'' policy was adopted by the Relief Committee until the family had reached the starvation level, and then the Royal Society for the Prevention of Cruelty to Children Officer was sent in to prosecute the father for neglect of his children.

But to continue the quotation from that sermon in St. Paul's: ''Is it unnatural that there grows steadily the feeling that they are in the grip of an inhuman machine over which they have no control? A feeling that nobody cares, that they are of no value in the world, unwanted? That, in fact, society would be glad if they did not exist? They are a problem, a nuisance, and they know you think so. Is that fair? Search your own hearts. How far is it true that you really think this of them—that the poor above everything else are a nuisance?

> For I tell you one thing success cannot stomach the sight of,
> And that's failure, the sort that you can't get away from or write off.
> But that shabbily, shamblingly, haunts you and cringes for pence,
> Am I wrong thus far, though I cause you offence?

"How far is it true that we are ashamed of the poor, and despise them? Or is it that our scorn is but a cover for our fear and our own shame? That we are not ashamed when they are meek and submissive, but if ever they dare to creep out of their hovels and flaunt their poverty in our faces, we jeer at them in our hearts, and secretly are glad if there is a disturbance and the police drive them back to submission and quiescence, for we can cover our own shame by saying, that, after all, it is only the agitator and truculent politician who is to blame?

"I tell you, my friends, that we who know them are glad when they show some signs of revolt, glad when some spark of resistance shows itself, glad when they dare to answer back. For to us it is a sign that they are not utterly despairing, but that there remains a spark of manhood, and that the sons of God are not so easily destroyed by adversity; a sign that the soul remains unconquered."

Because we felt so deeply on the matter, and in order to see what could be done from inside, Ethel Upton and I got ourselves put on the Public Assistance Committee, which had to work out the scales of relief and transitional benefit; and later on, when the Labour Party captured the L.C.C., both became chairmen of our respective Area Sub-committees. That change of leadership at County Hall made a great difference—the difference between those who were scaling down to give the least possible, and those who were striving to squeeze for the applicant for relief every shilling the law allowed, without facing another surcharging defeat.

I have often heard it said, "But does it matter much how you vote? Isn't one political party as bad as another?" Said, not in the optimistic way of a charming old lady of eighty on one polling day, who, in reply to my wife's question, "Are you going to vote?" said, "Oh yes, I'm going to give my vote; they does the best for us whoever they are"; but in the detached and cynical tones of a lay pillar of the Church, who at this period said, at an important gathering on social affairs, "Of course, no cultured person would dream of voting to-day". I have already described when I felt rather like that myself, when politics was to me rather like a game, with no real issues at stake. But now it had ceased to be a game. And when the L.C.C. was captured by the Labour Party, tied though they were by regulations which prevented them from doing much that they wanted to do, a great change came over the whole administrative machine.

Apart from the material benefits, the recipients of relief began to be treated as persons; and this new attitude showed itself in ways which in themselves may seem small, but which represented much to our people. "Brown" became "Mr. Brown" when he came before the Committee, and he was given a chair to sit on, instead of having to stand cap in hand while the inquisition on him and his family was being conducted. "Being treated as a person" is an important issue, particularly to those who are hanging on with their teeth to the last shreds of self-respect.

I remember Ethel Upton once telling me a story about Mr. ——, who had to appear before a certain Relieving Officer. She was in the next room, and heard a loud "Get out!" shouted by the Relieving Officer as Mr. —— went into the room, and the quiet shutting of the door as he went out again. This was repeated three times, followed the third time by "and remove your hat before you come in here".

"Oh, that's what's wrong," said Mr. ——. "Well, would

you mind taking off your hat when you come into my house, especially when my wife is present?''

The former attitude may seem strange to those who still think that ''courtesy'' is the prerogative of a public school education, but it is not so strange if you realise the situation. When G. D. H. Cole wrote those words I quoted in my St. Paul's sermon,

> For I tell you one thing success cannot stomach the sight of,
> And that's failure, the sort you can't get away from or write off.
> But that shabbily, shamblingly, haunts you and cringes for pence,

he was showing a real understanding of a common human heart, intensified by the feeling in the former ''public-school-tie'' administrators of relief, of hopelessness in the face of something they did not understand and which demanded a remedy comparable in sacrifice to that demanded by Jesus in the story of the rich young man, the camel and the needle's eye. Great riches in the midst of great poverty tends to create such divisions between persons that the fellowship which God demands becomes almost impossible. Few are capable of facing the cost of reconciliation.

Underneath, too, there lurked a fear of revolt. Over and over again, in discussing both imperialism and social reform, I have heard it said that the only way to prevent this was by keeping such people in constant dread of the consequences if they did so revolt, and a continuous sense of inferiority. I am sure that this method of making the unemployed feel inferior was part of a general tactic adopted through all these years. We were no longer allowed to march direct to Hyde Park, but were directed into roundabout ways. We were no longer allowed to hold meetings at our regular places, but were forced to hold them in out-of-the-way ones.

I remember once, after the order that ''no meetings of the unemployed must take place in the vicinity of the Labour

Exchanges'', though that seemed to us to be the natural meeting-place since they had anyway to hang about there much of the day, the unemployed announced a meeting in a road just off the Settles Street Exchange. The Inspector informed them that they could not hold it there. I was sent for, and, of course, offered to speak. I arrived to find a huge crowd gathered and a large force of police in attendance.

We began our meeting, only to be rushed by the police some thirty yards down the street to the next corner, where we were allowed to continue. I can remember now the rough gist of my speech: ''Chief Inspector, we wanted our meeting at that corner, you made us come here instead. If we had called it here, you would have made us go there. It does not matter to us whether we are here or there, but it does matter to you that where we speak shall be a matter for your decision, not ours. Comrades, I am saying this in your hearing, because I want you to realise what is happening. If you know what is happening and why it is happening, you won't let it break your spirits, and that is what matters most. They don't want you to feel that you are persons with the right to make real decisions for yourselves. They want you to feel that you have no will of your own, for they are afraid of what will happen if you begin to act as persons. Don't let any of these things destroy your self-respect, and the knowledge that each one of you matters, because you are a child of God. If you lose that, you lose everything. If you retain that, one day you will win through, and people will again treat you as men and women who matter.''

So we fought to keep alive that sense of being persons who mattered in those who were in most danger of losing it; and, whatever else this change of political leadership at County Hall meant, the change reflected itself naturally in personal relationships. For these new leaders rose mainly from their own ranks, and at least from their own movement. But, whether it was we or they, the administrative method itself was wrong, and no mere changes in personnel could undo the suffering it caused to thousands of families.

"Abolish the Means Test" became the most popular slogan, for under these conditions the Means Test became the epitome of their sufferings. I do not think that anything has contributed more to break up family life in the East End than that Means Test: nothing has done more to destroy the authority of the parents and their natural leadership. I well remember the bitter cry of a woman at an open-air meeting at which I was speaking. I was talking about unemployment, and a woman kept calling out: "There's only one solution, there's only one solution," till I was driven to ask "I wish, madam, you would tell us what the solution is", and received the reply "Birth control. There is no solution but birth control. We'll make them work themselves or give us work." Knowing this attitude and the increasing spread of the use of contraceptives because of the fear of bringing children into that sort of world, it was particularly galling to me to hear the constant gibe that the unemployed brought more children into the world in order to increase their allowances.

The pittance they received for each child at school was anyway not sufficient to keep them; and as soon as the children left school and went to work, many of them were driven to leave home and to lodge in the next street, in order to save their parents and themselves from the Means Test. It was this which contributed much to the exodus of so many girls from South Wales and Durham, and their desperate descent on London. The boys, of course, could find work till they were eighteen; but after that age they gradually found themselves on the streets, lounging at street corners and trying desperately to avoid Belmont.

Belmont! How the name stinks in the nostrils of the workers still in the East End! I remember my own fury when I first went on the Area Sub-committee and heard Belmont used as a threat. "If you don't find work soon, I'll send you to Belmont."

"The training camp", it was called. I went there once to see the men being "trained". Building houses inside a shed with mud and bricks, and then knocking them down again to begin again with the same mud and bricks; knowing that at the end of it all they had not a dog's chance of helping to build a proper house, though God knows they needed them badly enough; brush-makers out of work learning to make brushes, and this time for institutions for which they had made brushes as free men before they became unemployed, and which now, by taking the brushes made in Belmont, were keeping them out of work. It is true that many officials there were trying desperately to make life more tolerable for the men and to give them interesting work to do. But under those conditions, with men there against their will, regarding Belmont in their own words as a "slave camp", they could do little to break down the hate or the fear of it. No one went to Belmont willingly. Yet to revolt against Belmont meant being forced to leave home, or endangering the whole family, who were not allowed to provide food for those who revolted; and the threat of action by the R.S.P.C.C. was a constant fear. There were many who tried it once, and then no more. They drifted about and stood on street corners. Boys that we knew as healthy youngsters once—leaving school eager to work—now becoming loungers and scroungers because society had no use for them.

It didn't stop there. In such a situation petty crime began to increase, and the old law of "loitering to commit a felony" was resurrected to deal with it. Any young man loitering about, particularly after dark, became liable to arrest on sight, and to conviction on the evidence that he seemed to be acting suspiciously and was unemployed.

In my ignorance I did not know, till I attended a police court, that a man's record could be read out before deciding the question of guilt. I thought that that was withheld until it came to the amount of sentence. But I soon found out what a crime it was to be unemployed. It was not till I had protested against what to me was an injustice that the magistrate said to me: "Petty crime is increasing in the East End.

It is obviously this kind of person who is responsible. They have no visible means of support and must be making their living somehow. Whether a man is unemployed and has no visible means of support or not is evidence that must be used to support or contradict the police statement.''

I once heard that magistrate say in the open court, when he dismissed two young men, to one of them: ''There seems to have been a mistake here. This young man has a steady job and a good home. He doesn't seem to be in any need, or to have any motive for stealing. Case dismissed''; and to the other: ''You may think yourself lucky, young man, to be caught with somebody who seems to have no motive for stealing.'' It all sounds fantastic now. But it didn't seem so to people then, in spite of our attempts to rouse public opinion.

The whole question was argued out at some length in a High Court test case, when it was decided that if a group existed who were a danger to the community it was not sufficient in the first instance to prove that a man belonged to that group as conclusive of guilt that he intended to commit a felony; there must be a previous occasion for suspicion. The case was reported in full in the *Times Law Report* of 30th October 1936: ''Ledwith and another *v.* Roberts and another.'' In the course of that appeal Lord Justice Greene said: ''It is beyond dispute that there was, in our earlier history, an unemployed class which was only too well known and always regarded as a public menace, and that it was this class which was intended by all the expressions 'idle and disorderly persons', 'persons using loitering', 'rogues and vagabonds', and 'sturdy beggars'. That the class was treated as semi-criminal is also beyond argument; they were referred to by such phrases as 'outrageous enemies to the common weal' . . . When the London Act of 1839 was passed the phrase 'loose, idle, and disorderly' persons must, in my view, be presumed to have been used by Parliament in the same sense as before—namely, as applying to an unemployed idle class, given to preying on those who worked or were possessed of other means. . . .

"It seems to me wrong," he continued, "that these old phrases should still be made the occasion of arrest and prosecution, when in their historical meaning they are so utterly out of keeping with modern life in England. . . . Is it not time that our relevant statutes should be revised and that punishment and arrest should no longer depend on words which to-day have an uncertain sense and which nobody can truly apply to modern conditions? To retain such laws seems to me inconsistent with our national sense of personal liberty or our respect for the rule of law."

Nevertheless, in spite of that expression of opinion by a High Court Judge, the arrests went on. There had to be a previous occasion of suspicion! I remember being in the court a few days later when a man who was being examined was told beforehand to plead this judgement. The conversation went something like this.

The policeman stated when and where he had seen the man loitering:

Magistrate: What have you to say?

Defendant: I plead Ledwith and Roberts.

Magistrate to the Policeman: What have you to say to that?

Policeman: That means there must be a previous occasion. Well, I saw him about an hour before in the same place acting suspiciously.

Magistrate: An hour before. I think we had better adjourn the case and take advice on that.

What a farce it was! But its repercussions on the unemployed were immense, and often I have had men come to me and say that they had to be careful whenever they walked about the streets at night. Even my own churchwarden—a boiler-maker—was held up one night, when he was coming home with his tool-bag on his shoulder, and forced to accompany the policeman to a telephone booth to ring up and prove that he was in the job he said he was. You see, he had been unemployed, but, unknown to the police, he had started work again.

But why walk the streets at night? I remember one night I was woken up at about 3 a.m. by a man who had walked all the way from Poplar. I let him in, and sat down expecting some dreadful tale, only to hear: "Father John, please tell me who was the Pharaoh who built the Pyramids?" He then burst into tears, and continued: "I'm sorry, but I sometimes think this unemployment will drive me mad. I lie awake at night and think and think because I can't sleep; and then some perfectly silly thing like this gets into my brain, and I must know the answer or I feel I'll lose my reason." We had a short talk. He refused a cup of tea, because he thought it would give me too much trouble, and off he went quite cheerfully on the long walk back to Poplar.

But—to turn from this to another side of it all—housing. Stepney was, of course, a black spot—one of the worst in London. We are apt to forget how bad it was. I remember during the war an occasion when an exalted person, described to me as "the second lady in the land", came to look at some of our shelters under the railway arches. She was horror-struck with the conditions there, but amazed at the cheerfulness of the people, and said to me: "I can't understand how these people keep so cheerful under such conditions; they're wonderful." In reply I took her outside and showed her some of the houses still standing there. "Do you see those houses? We've been fighting for years to have them condemned. They are damper than the arches; they swarm with rats and vermin. The arches have no rats and fewer vermin. In those houses the people have been sleeping more than two in a bed for years; in the arches they have a bed each. In those arches, bad as they are, some of the people are better off than they were in peacetime. They learned how to endure in peacetime, and it became a habit to stick almost anything." It is only fair to add that, at times during the war, the shelter conditions were terrible—most of them were hurried improvisations—and also that a casual visitor, particularly a V.I.P., rarely saw the results of them on the people's morale. I remember one particularly bad shelter, which I reported to the Home Secretary as very damaging, not only to health, but to public morale (the latter I mentioned because it sometimes took the threat of that to get quick attention). He sent a V.I.P. down to enquire. When he arrived, the people who normally sat about and grumbled in a most dejected manner all got up and cheered like mad. He went back and reported that there was nothing wrong with morale, and everybody was happy. Consequently nothing was done. I again reported this matter as urgent, but this time took the precaution of telling the people that when the next V.I.P. came they were to behave normally. He was correspondingly shocked; and within forty-eight hours a squad of workmen arrived to deal with the shelter.

But to return to housing. Sometimes people talk now as though this question of bad and inadequate housing had only just cropped up. The damage that the war did in the East End by bombing has obliterated pre-war memories. They forget those days before the bombing, days when materials were plentiful and builders unemployed.

I remember, when I first came to Poplar, meeting a man who lived in a room ten feet by six off St. Leonard's Road with his wife and two children, and hearing: "It's good to have a home of your own at last." I said: "But man, where have you been living?" and he replied: "On boxes in the passage." That was five years after the first world war in an East End comparatively undamaged.

In 1929 a Committee of the Church in the Deanery of Stepney, presided over by the Rev. R. A. Edwards of St. Faith's, reported as follows:

"The 1921 Census showed that there were 62,921 people in Stepney living more than two per room, 184 more than six per room, and 3,697 houses occupied by three or more families. . . . It is difficult to make plain in writing what a slum home really means. There is an opening here for a novelist of conviction and sympathy. In the first place it should be remembered that a slum home consists in the majority of cases of one or two rooms only. The rooms themselves may be in any sort of condition from extreme dilapidation to, comparatively speaking, a good state of repair; and generally they are, in view of all the circumstances, wonderfully clean and well kept. The rooms are always small, and usually each contains at least one bed. In some cases there is not room for the whole family ever to have a meal together. Sleeping arrangements are always difficult. Sometimes the girls will be put into one of the rooms, while the boys sleep behind a curtain in the room occupied by their parents. Children are born in these conditions, and the various stages of life are passed there. There is no privacy of any kind. A bath is a matter of extreme difficulty. The W.C. is in the yard, and there is usually only one per house. There is rarely more than one tap. A death inflicts a dreadful inconvenience. The coffin must be kept until the funeral in one or other of the rooms or in the undertaker's stable. Life and all its affairs is, in a slum home, a very public thing, in which much of the proper decency and ordinary reticence of behaviour is impossible.''

It was over housing that we fought some of our fiercest battles between 1937 and 1939, and in those battles something of the old spirit began to return. I sometimes think that, if the war had not come when it did, that revolt would have been the prelude to the overthrow of the Government. The Means Test had already done much to destroy family life, but this growing menace bid fair to destroy home life altogether. For a working man to lose his house is to lose everything. The rent had to be paid even at the cost of food, and the rents were rising rapidly as the decontrolling acts began to take cumulative effect. Normally the Public Assistance Committee could not allow more than 15s. a week for rent for those on relief; but the landlord was demanding more and more, sometimes for houses with boarded-up windows and doors off their hinges, ceilings down, and rain coming in. Yet they had to pay, and the money had to come from the allowance we made for food, though that was already reckoned on the bare subsistence level. To refuse was to run the risk of arrears and eviction; to lose their house was to lose the right to outdoor relief altogether. So they paid whatever was demanded, and the family went short of necessary food. The fear of the landlord was added to the other anxieties.

But, even when they managed to pay, there seemed no way of forcing the landlord to keep the property in decent repair. At first we tried to work within the law. We helped individuals and gave them advice; we called in the sanitary inspectors; we threatened landlords with exposure; in one case the whole of our Church Council at Watney Street threatened to blockade ourselves inside one home to force the landlord to repair a roof when the snow lay on the children's beds; later we took over one house and withheld the rent to pay for the repairs which we were undertaking ourselves, so as to force the landlord to take legal action against us. But it was slow work, and it soon became obvious that such methods were merely playing with the problem. So we came together—an organisation of tenants which ignored party divisions—only to find within the space of a few weeks that we could not cope with the crowds coming for help and advice. The queues lengthened, till we were kept at it till midnight day after day. We found that the existing law allowed no redress for the de-controlled tenants, nor could we bring any real pressure on the landlords to do the necessary repairs by individual action. So we formed our Tenants' League, and began to organise on a large scale.

This is no place to write a history of those two pre-war years. I cannot praise too highly the work which Tubby Rosen and Michael Shapiro, two Communists, put into it till the war came and we found ourselves in different camps, as they were forced to take the "party line" on that issue. Nor can I tell you how we got tenants at first in the large blocks of flats to organise together, controlled and de-controlled, and present common demands; how we interviewed landlords and tried to settle directly; how eventually we were forced to withhold rents or collect them ourselves and hold them till our conditions were accepted; how almost miraculously the organisation spread, till it was covering whole areas of Stepney and began to join up with similar movements in Poplar and elsewhere.

I don't think we ever lost a strike. Sometimes in the early days we came across cases where the real landlord had never seen the property from which he drew his rents, and our actions forced him to come and see for himself and realise with horror the conditions for which his negligence was responsible. The organisation spread from blocks of flats to streets, which were far more difficult to organise and brought us more directly into antagonism with the ground landlords, who thought they could escape responsibility.

I have often been asked since then whether it was true that our difficulties were due to the fact that the landlords were Jews and that it was all a Jewish racket. That was not so. There were Jewish landlords, of course, but there were also Gentile; there were city companies and individuals; the ground landlords were sometimes bankers, and, in one particularly nauseous case which I remember, a knight of high repute who was chairman of many Christian philanthropic concerns. No, the whole thing had grown up and was intertwined with the rotting system in which it had its origin. No one seemed responsible, and many individuals, who expressed concern, found themselves so tied by their own entanglements with others that they could not free themselves. There had been loans, there had been bankruptcies, there were interested third parties, there were complications of all sorts; but, in the whole of our experience, we never came across a single instance of those cases which certain M.P.s and Press organs talked about—poor lone widows who had invested their savings in houses and to whose sufferings we were adding.

It was all a vast tangle of interests, complicated by the fact that the hint of rebuilding and of requisitioning of property for that purpose caused such speculation that some of the worst property was changing hands constantly and fetching a higher price at each transaction. Each speculator hoped for profit of a kind that the Archbishop of Canterbury once likened to "profit on stinking fish". I remember well one block of houses, one room up, one down, four feet between the front door and a high wall and no water save from a tap in a yard. We insisted on the reduction of those rents to 10s. a week; in reality, so filthy, rat- and vermin-ridden were they that the inmates should have been paid to live in them. The landlord told us almost in tears he could not stand this reduction. He had only "just bought them on the understanding that the L.C.C. were going to buy" and had paid a high price in consequence, only to find that they were just outside the proposed clearance area.

Nothing could cut through this maze of muddle and financial interests and end this suffering but large-scale action ready to face the uproar which action would cause. Two things amazed me about those strikes and amaze me still when I look back.

One was the speed with which people came together, organised, and threw up their own leaders, in spite of all they had gone through and the years in which they seemed so apathetic. Once shown a possible way out of at least one of their problems, they jumped to it, and showed an ability for organisation, for persistency, adaptability, and self-sacrifice which astounded all the critics. The women—married women with families—were the backbone of it all: they seemed to have found at last a way by which they could emulate the feats of their men who had suffered and fought in the early days of the building up of trade unionism. They ran great risks. In one case, where blocks of flats with over two hundred families were on strike, they actually resisted a siege of months behind barbed wire, and shopped, and cooked, and took turns at picket duty day and night under such conditions. And this in London in 1938!

The second thing which amazed us all was their neighbourliness. In one case of over three hundred families, the majority of whom were living in flats where the rents were controlled and therefore capable of legal adjustment, the whole lot came out to defend the rights of the minority, who were de-controlled and at the mercy of the landlords. After months of struggle they were prepared to accept a settlement which gave them their original demands—justice for the minority. While they did secure for themselves, as for others, proper repair of the whole buildings, they never wavered from their original demands about rent, in spite of all they had suffered and risked.

Perhaps that rekindling of hope and comradeship had more to do with the winning of the war than many now realise. Certainly it came just in time to restore the morale of the people.

But this was the situation in 1938-9, twenty years after the end of the first war, when the Government began with resources which to-day we would give anything to possess; began in a world with a still workable economy; with a country which had not suffered from bombing, or a Europe in ruins; began with huge overseas assets still realisable.

Twenty years after the Armistice, with millions of unemployed, millions still living in houses unfit for human habitation, millions hungry and badly clothed, with the shops and warehouses stuffed with goods which the hungry could not buy, with shoemakers out of work and their children unshod because they had made too many shoes! Bellamy's parable of the water-tank which the workers had filled with water which they were unable to drink because they had no money, while they were not allowed to earn money because there was too much water, had become literal truth.

Think back, and compare our situation now with that of twenty years after the first war. In a crisis incomparably worse than that, the masses with all their present deprivations are fed and clothed better, and have a feeling of self-respect which, if we could be transported back to those evil 'thirties, would look like heaven.

It is important that we should be aware of what this means

in relation to the task which now lies ahead of us. I sometimes wonder what would have happened if the war had not come when it did. Things were pretty desperate. It is just possible that the workers would have turned to open revolutionary activity and looked to the Communist Party for leadership. Certainly there were a great many who were thinking that way, and looking in that direction for guidance. It is precisely in such a situation, and only in such a situation, that both history and Communist theory teach us that the steady evolutionary process gives way to violent and sudden revolutionary activity. If people, driven to desperation, are left with such activity as the only way to throw off the yoke of tyrants, I know of nothing in the Christian faith which would condemn them. But we have always hoped that in Britain there was a better way of bringing about vital social changes. The sort of society which we have always striven for is one which can neither be imposed from above nor be the result of a deprivation of vital material things, which brings in its train a violent upsurge of revolt. By its very nature and activity such a revolt tends to submerge many of the values which are essential to that society.

While we have always recognised that the worker in desperation might be driven to take such action, we have always hoped not only that the desire for that new life, but the readiness to pay the cost of its achievement was something which would come willingly and instinctively out of the heart of a people aflame with a faith that springs from the Christian democratic tradition in which our movement has its roots. It would come, that is, not out of despair, but out of faith and hope and love; not in a moment of desperation, but at a time when we willed it because we believed in it, and were ready to work and sacrifice for it because we willed it.

But in spite of all their sufferings the masses generally were still far from accepting the Communist philosophy, however much at times they tended to look to it for leadership. It was true that they were driven more and more to an acceptance of the Marxian interpretation of events and that fewer went to church; but they still wished their children to be brought up as Christians, they still believed in God, they still believed that a human being had both rights and duties which come to him because he is a child of God and not a mere animal scrabbling for his existence; they still knew that the death of the body was not the end of them or their loved ones. Though they knew that there were many Communists who had been in the past and who would in the future prove true friends and allies; that they were valiant fighters, self-sacrificing to a degree in a cause in which they believed; that many of them called themselves Communists because they loved their fellow men and saw no other way of freeing them; that many of them had been driven to deny God and oppose the Church because so many of those who profess a love for God deny their profession by their cruelty to their fellow men; nevertheless, in spite of all this, they could never go Communist unless all other hope had gone. Then, indeed, they might be driven there.

If a Government came into power which treated them again as it did in those 'thirties, if it tried to force them again to poverty and degradation, then I believe they might be driven to accept a way and a leadership which would contradict the whole history of the British working-class movement. That is, I believe, what might have happened in 1939 if the war had not come. The history of these years helps also to explain the attitude of many who did join the Communist Party and who at the dictation of the Comintern, and against their will, took their stand with Russia in refusing to join in the struggle against Hitler. Such men never believed that those who had helped Hitler into power and condoned the excesses of Mussolini, and who, even at the last moment, were actively engaged in trying to push them off at other people's expense, were true in their determination to fight. They saw and judged their rulers in the light of their responsibility for those years of suffering at home. In this situation they believed they were matching opportunism with opportunism.

Those of us who tried so hard to prevent Munich, and who had laboured to get Great Britain and France to join in a pact with Russia against Hitler, could never join in the chorus of hate which followed the Russian-German pact. We believed that the Russians only signed that agreement when they had been persuaded by our past diplomacy and our present vacillation that Great Britain and France were willing to turn Hitler eastwards again as they had done at Munich.

We believed that they were wrong; for though that pact gave them a short breathing-space, it lengthened the war. But it did more. The subsequent public distortion of truth by Soviet Russia, the open flattery by it of men guilty of such wholesale cruelty as the Nazi leaders, and the acceptance of that position by the British Communist Party, revealed, as nothing hitherto had done, the deep gulf between them and the mass of the British working class, who have never been able to accept their doctrine that the end justifies the means.

4
THE CHALLENGE TO CHRISTIANITY

IT will, of course, be argued that the account given above is an over-simplification, and, to some extent, an exaggerated picture. Admittedly most of my illustrations come out of my own personal experiences and contacts. But I do not believe that they will be contradicted by the experience of others in close contact with other large industrial areas. Not only so, but the germs both of these conditions, and of the ideas resulting from them, were to be found in a great number of rural districts.

But there is more to it than this. This festering sore has to be seen in its setting within the whole body. It is indicative of disease within that whole body, however much this or that individual member was or was not yet aware of its effects on him. The modern world is so closely interrelated in every respect that phrases like "peace is indivisible" are not merely pious commonplaces, but possess a real meaning.

We may not yet have reached the stage where "from the sole of the foot even unto the head there is no soundness at all, but wounds and bruises and putrefying sores; they have not been closed, neither bound up, neither mollified with ointment" (*Isa*. 1. 6). For that God is to be thanked. Nevertheless, there was sufficient putrefaction to make "the whole head sick and the whole heart faint", because health of the body is indivisible, and chronic disease in any part cannot help but communicate itself to every part and make "the whole heart faint".

That is to say, all over Britain, wherever I travelled, in universities not less than in other places, a creeping paralysis could be discerned, revealing itself in a feeling of impotence and frustration coupled with anxiety as to the future. People were becoming more and more callous to human suffering as a result of its very magnitude and to their inability to do anything about it. The problem was too vast and complicated. So they tended to shut themselves in their little compartments, hoping against hope that the world would right itself; concentrating in the meantime on saving what they could of life for themselves and their families. The effect of all this on themselves and on their religious and social outlook was very great. It would have been disastrous had not something like the war torn them from this attempt at insularity, and thrown them willy-nilly into the maelstrom of world affairs.

Nor can we escape responsibility for that situation at home by pointing to worse things happening elsewhere. Archbishop William Temple said in 1937 that "The springs of humanity are being dried up by continual pressure of horror upon horror, and we are in danger of becoming case-hardened. There is a real risk in times like these of a great backward step on the part of mankind. . . . I have been amazed that the thing that took place not long ago in Addis Ababa has gone by without a howl of rage from the whole of the civilised world." But that howl of rage did not come. It would have been hypocritical if it had come from a people trying to shut its eyes to things happening on its own doorstep, for which it had a more immediate responsibility and about which it could have acted with real effect.

That, then, was the position in 1939, and it is well for us to take careful stock of it. It is our duty to try to see why we had got into it, and why the various groups within the nation acted as they did, if we are to avoid a similar situation in the future.

Why is it that people subject to such conditions become an easy prey to the materialist's argument that all this religious talk about the value of the individual person is just claptrap? Is it to be wondered at that they cease to come to church or to associate themselves publicly with "religion"?

To people in such a case, feeling that they no longer matter as persons, with no say at all in how life is organised, it does seem that, in fact, the dignity and value of a person is determined by his place in society or the use that someone in power has for him. A lucky gamble, and men's status changes; people take notice of them and they are treated as persons. What more natural than that they should turn to one or other of those new creeds which offered them, while they were still nobodies, some sense of worth and dignity as members of a victorious class or race?

If so many of them did not succumb either openly or furtively to this, it is due to the fact that there is in man a "givenness" which no external conditions can completely obliterate. No matter how great the external bombardment on their minds, no matter how great the material deprivation, every effort either to fit them into a mould, or to subject them to conditions which seem to be completely destructive of personality, is eventually destroyed on the rock of this "givenness of man"; on the fact that "God breathed into his nostrils the breath of life and man became a living soul"; on the fact of God's love and the continuance of His redeeming activity in the world. Julius Hecker once said in the middle of the Russian revolution that if it were possible to destroy completely in a people the sense of their "otherness" it would be a proof of the non-existence of God.

But if throughout this picture—terrible as it is—we can look back with pride to the homes alive with love, to the self-sacrifice and devotion of parents and children, to the men and women of our streets who maintained their dignity and self-respect in spite of all those things which humanly speaking should have destroyed them, don't let us also belittle for one moment the power of environment and material conditions so to mould the minds and outlook of whole peoples as to determine the destiny of nations. The history of Europe between the wars is surely sufficient to warn us against such complacency.

But—to return to the other side of the picture—how comes

it about that people of wealth and culture, people in whose homes there is obviously so much love and self-sacrifice and virtue, how can they live in comparative comfort and even luxury in the midst of such misery, and seem not to care? How can their leaders and representatives be guilty of so heartless a policy? How is it, indeed, that human beings on either side of the fence can approach the mental attitude described by G. D. H. Cole in one of his poems on the Means Test?

Because you look well fed and sleek,
    I hate you.
Because you've a regular income every week,
    I hate you.
Because you are strong and proud, and I am weak,
    I hate you.
Because you expect me to be humble and meek,
    I hate you.
Because of superiority you reek,
    I hate you.
I hate you because you dole me out my pittance
As if of all human claims it were more than quittance.
God, if only I could afford to fling your dole
Back in your ugly face, and save my soul,
I should have no need to hate you—you and your charity.

That's what the unemployed man didn't say
When the Public Assistance Committee assessed his pay,
But that's what his soul said. Now, for the sake of parity,
Let's try to put down, with no less brutal clarity,
What the sleek and superior Chairman said in his soul,
As he fixed the amount of the claimant's weekly dole.

Because you look poor and down at heel,
    I hate you.
Because my money you'd like to steal,
    I hate you.

Because you're a danger to the Commonweal,
    I hate you.
Because you make me ashamed of my next square meal,
    I hate you.
Because I don't want to know what you feel,
    I hate you.
I hate you because I've got to pay for your subsistence.
I hate you because there's no reason for your existence.
I suppose I've got to keep you and your brats from starvation,
Or else you'll be breaking windows. Hell and damnation,
Why did I ever take on this job? I hate it.

That's the other side of the case, as I have to state it.
For that's what the Chairman of the Public Assistance Committee,
A man exceedingly well thought of in the City,
Didn't say as he told the claimant, who'd been unemployed
Three years on the dole, his skill at his trade destroyed,
He'd have to manage on two bob less, now the nation
Was reduced to a state of complete financial prostration.
Which done, he went off to his club, and made a good dinner,
And it never even occurred to him that he was the sinner.[1]

Those of my readers who think that we have never yet reached that state in Britain will, at least, agree that it has been reached in Italy, Spain, Germany, Russia and elsewhere. Is the answer simply that some people are worse than others, or that some races are more backward than others? Or, are there some contributory causes which are as discernible here as elsewhere, but which have not as yet been so continuously or so insistently operative?

To bring the matter really home: how is it that people so pleasant personally—politicians, business men and women, leading Christians and others of repute, could support a policy which allowed this sort of thing to continue, and

[1] G. D. H. Cole, *The Crooked World*, p. 22.

seem to regard the sufferings it entailed so callously?

They seem to take for granted their right to govern, their right to power and privilege, their right to immense personal possessions carrying with them a right to employ people when it pays and dismiss them when it ceases to pay, their right to regulate the whole productive and distributive machine in relation to personal profit, and not primarily for the needs of society as a whole, and resent any restrictions on their doing so. When, as a result of this iniquitous theory, they are forced to deal with those who suffer deprivation, they reverse the consistent Christian ethical principle which regards the relief of necessity as the payment of a debt, not a "charity", on the grounds that in the presence of riches "the poor are poor because they have been robbed".[1] On the whole, they believe that the poor are poor because they are indigent, and relieve themselves of responsibility by a comfortable twist of the words "ye have the poor always with you". Confront them with a case of individual necessity, and often they give generously; but confront them with an issue which challenges their assumptions, and they turn away contemptuously.

Of course, there are numerous instances of individuals who think and act otherwise, sometimes at great cost to themselves and their families; but as a class, and legislating as a class, they regard the maintenance of the present order with its priorities as the will of God. They are confirmed in that belief by the attitude of a great many representative Christians who take refuge in what they consider to be a "disinterested neutrality", and give as an excuse that a Christian should not meddle in politics, or at least that the "Church" should not do so—a principle which, however admirable in theory, commits them as officials to the support of the *status quo* and in general to a denunciation of those who rebel against it.

When Charles Kingsley said that "Religion is an opiate to keep the people quiet" this is what he meant. When my

[1] See p. 27 above.

little Russian barber talked about equating "God" and "the Czar" this is what he meant. When I was talking to a group of representative German Christians in Geneva before the war about a possible resistance to Hitler I was met continually with the statement "The Church's concern is spiritualities. It is the duty of the State to concern itself with politics. Hitler is the head of the State, and we are bound to support him even to the extent of going to war", and it took the whole course of the atrocities, and the war itself, to convince them of their guilt in so doing.

It is undeniable that there is a widespread effort on the part of the Church to move away from this theory, which has never, of course, been representative of the best minds in the Church through the centuries. When leading Christians really get down to consider the matter objectively they produce such documents as the Reports of Copec, the Archbishop's Report on Industry in 1919, the findings of the Malvern Conference, and the various Encyclicals of the Roman Pontiff. But why is it that the Hammonds, while they can point to minds for whom "Christianity provides a standard by which to judge government, the industrial and economic order, the life of society, the way in which it distributes wealth and opportunities",[1] can yet make the generalisation that "The history of the English Church in the eighteenth century is one aspect of the history of a class",[2] and that "The English Church accepted the position that religion was, in fact, part of the civil constitution of society. It knew its place in the domestic establishments of the State, and it took its colour for good and for evil from the world of the ruling class"?[3]

But to come nearer to our own day. It is surely a pertinent criticism of the Church in Italy before the war that, in the various crises which faced her, she was so concerned for her own status and self-preservation as an organisation that she

[1] J. L. and B. Hammond, *The Town Labourer*, p. 224.
[2] ibid., p. 222.
[3] ibid., p. 275.

was prepared to sacrifice truth and honour and acquiesce in the most flagrant injustices, rather than risk crucifixion or the confiscation of her property and deprivation of her privileges.

In Spain, in spite of noble instances to the contrary, the body of the hierarchy gave active support to General Franco, not because he represented a higher and better conception of life and justice, but because, by so doing, they safeguarded the Church's worldly possessions, her national status, and the whole set of privileges which had grown up during the alliance of Church and State in that country.

In England, every large-scale religious organisation, whether established or not, has in modern times become so tied up in the social order with which their privileges, power, and economic independence are inextricably bound up that their leaders have tended to equate the decision of the governing body of that order with the will of God.

While, as individuals, they have no doubt been shocked by the horrors in the world, as organisations they have tended to hide behind the same network of lies and hypocrisy as their civil rulers, and to turn blind eyes to such facts as were inconvenient. So they became, in fact, responsible for the train of events during those inter-war years, which not only involved our own people in such suffering, but which led eventually to the slaughter of war.

The refusal of the Church to insist on those principles and that life to which she was created to witness has involved her in a terrible responsibility for the present situation. When the Church ceases to be the guardian of truth, and justice, and right human relationships, she becomes the handmaid of expediency. In a situation in which untold millions were available at any moment for armaments, in which luxury abounded in one section of society and another section was subject to conditions which were an insult to Christ in the person of His poor, the Church seemed officially to acquiesce in a scale of values and priorities which are a reversal of those of Christ.

The continuance of large-scale unemployment depriving millions of their proper status in society, the housing conditions which subjected millions of our people to such hardship at a time when money and labour were both available in almost unlimited quantities: these and other things have indeed evoked from time to time dignified and restrained criticism. But nothing was said or done officially likely to destroy our respectability, or lower our prestige, or damage us as an institution, in the eyes of the "powers that be". Yet what a howl of protest would have risen officially, and from us all in this country, if Church property were to be attacked on a large scale, or the parson's freehold threatened, or the general condition of life of those who live by the Church brought within measurable distance of the lives of those whose conditions I have attempted to describe.

Is it difficult to understand why this should be so? Is it not natural that all large-scale institutions, including the Church, should become so intertwined with the existing order, so bound in thought and action by their environment, with buildings to preserve and keep up, with staffs to pay, and invested finances, with families of their own to provide for and the future to take into account, that they come to feel that they depend on the preservation of that social order? Indeed, it has seemed so obvious that when vital decisions affecting the lives of the whole of society were made the ruling classes have generally taken for granted that they could carry the Church with them as an ally, because they believed that the same reasons which impelled them to such decisions would also be determinative of Church policy.

I have used the situation of the Church to illustrate my point, because I want to show that a particular determinative principle is operative even in the sphere where we should least expect to find it. We cannot explain all this merely in terms of the natural sinfulness of the individual man. Archbishop Temple in his Penguin, *Christianity and Social Order*, after discussing the "doctrine of original sin", goes on to show how we are concerned here with more than individuals and individual sins.[1] The whole matter becomes more complicated the moment the individual becomes involved in society, as he is bound to be. Man is a social animal; and in history he is bound to associate himself with other persons. In order to live at all he has to work out some sort of organisation to cover the various activities which are necessary to make social life possible. This is not selfishness, but necessity. If, as the Archbishop says, man tends to see things as good or bad primarily as they affect him personally, so he tends to regard the preservation of these necessary social organisations, with which his life is bound up, as the criterion for judging anything which impinges on them. The original associations he forms have, no doubt, an element of sin in them from the beginning—an element of exclusive self-assertion—but quite possibly they are at that moment the best form of organisation he can devise to meet his social needs, and suit the nation admirably. In that sense they are good. But before long the individual finds himself so involved in them that he is unable to free himself. So conditioned is he by them that he is unable to rise to the occasion when a new adaptation becomes necessary in changed circumstances, or a challenge comes from outside which demands an objective judgement on his part on that whole organisation of life by which he lives, and which he has for so long taken for granted as good.

Perhaps it is easiest to explain how deep this tendency goes if we look at the story of the Crucifixion of Jesus, and consider what light it throws on this challenge of God to man in history. When Jesus came to "save men from their sins" He seemed to have recognised and reckoned with both this individual sinfulness and the way in which men, acting with quite good motives, build for themselves organisations and associations which initially serve good and lawful purposes, but which in time enchain them and render them incapable of objective judgement. In particular, we notice that He predicted that He would be crucified in Jerusalem and no-

[1] *Christianity and Social Order*, p. 36 f.

where else. He knew that sooner or later His life must culminate in a challenge to the authorities there. When the time came He deliberately entered Jerusalem and forced a decision. He must do so in Jerusalem, not because these men were in themselves better or worse than other men, but because they were in the seats of authority, and represented the central organisation of the life of that day. Their decision affected the whole of organised society, and if Jesus were to save His people from their sins He must challenge sin not merely as it showed itself in individuals, but in the sort of life and organisation which sinful man had built. In this we see the true nature of sin. It cannot be otherwise, for life is both social and sacramental.

There, in Jerusalem, were men who alone could speak for society as a whole, and make executive decisions which affected the individuals who composed it. To understand why these particular people were there, and why they acted as they did, it is necessary to go back into the whole history of races and creeds and to discover the good and the evil, the endeavours, sins, and mistakes, of whole peoples. These men represented that which men had so built. They acted as interpreters of a way of life which Jesus must challenge and expose at its real worth, in the light of truth. Jesus not only challenged it, but knew beforehand the result of that challenge, because He knew that men in such positions are so tied and bound that their decisions are almost automatic when the challenge is such that it is a threat to their "world".

In such a situation men seem to act almost as puppets on a stage at the mercy of group desires and group alliances, which are the result of far more than their individual sins. The love and hate, prejudices, combinations, political, social, and religious concordats which went to form them, stretch right back into their history. So set and tied are they that it is only too often possible to plan with some certainty, believing they will act in a particular way under certain given circumstances. So Jesus could anticipate the result of His challenge and plan accordingly.

Caiaphas and the High Priests were not only the official representatives of the best and most advanced religion of their day, but the rulers of the nation as well. In that double capacity they were vitally concerned for the preservation of that religion and the Jewish race with which it was so closely bound up. They had come to an understanding with the Romans with that in mind. To them, the preservation of that concordat was of vital importance for their religious and social purposes. There was a real danger, to their minds, that both the nation and the "Church" would be destroyed if they supported Jesus. That "Church" and nation, which stood for religion, must at all costs be safeguarded.

Jesus Himself had warned His disciples of the danger of persecution and death at the hands of those "who thought they were doing God's service".

These leaders stated their case quite clearly. "If we let Him alone, all men will believe on Him, and the Romans will come and take away both our place and our nation"; to which Caiaphas added: "It is expedient that one man should die for the people that the whole nation perish not." It seems, too, perfectly clear that concern for "Church and nation" was so closely bound up with their own personal interests that the two were inseparable in their minds. Their own wealth and privileged position depended on that Roman concordat. Conflict with Rome would have meant the end of their comfort and security. The cleansing of the Temple by Jesus had threatened the source of that wealth and privilege, and Jesus had more than once drawn attention to the injustice of their commercial and legal transactions, and of the way in which their religious regulations were biased by the desire for financial gain. It seems obvious in the narrative of events that the safeguarding of that which they considered good, and their personal advantage in maintaining it, were so intertwined that they could not be separated in making a judgement on the challenge of Jesus.

When we turn to Pilate we see the same forces at work in the mind of the representative of the secular order. The

Roman Empire, which he represented, was probably the best and most just, as well as the most powerful, secular organisation in the world. There is no doubt that Pilate wanted to save Jesus. Privately, on this occasion anyway, although generally a harsh and brutal procurator, he showed a real desire to think objectively. But in the end he was forced to act as a person responsible for the maintenance of this concordat with the Jews and a keeper of the peace. He was obviously puzzled that people who had no love for the Romans should charge one of their own nation with sedition, and very surprised that, in view of that charge, they should prefer the release of another insurrectionist—Barabbas—to that of Jesus. ''Thine own nation hath delivered thee unto me; what hast thou done?'' Though he tried to rid himself of responsibility for the crucifixion by washing his hands of the matter, he was in the end forced to act as an official responsible for the maintenance of a concordat concluded by persons other than himself.

Yet again, so closely is that linked up with his own self-interest that St. John makes the cry ''If thou let this man go, thou art not Caesar's friend'' the decisive one.

As an historical fact it is not the worst men in history who order the crucifixion. The decision is made by people who stand for something good, and who are honestly concerned for the maintenance of a cause which, in their opinion, is a bulwark against anarchy and chaos. It is this idolatry, so natural to sinful man, which the Cross exposes, and which is being constantly exposed by God's judgement throughout human history. If in the course of history this idolatry is more obvious, and has far greater historical effect, in those who hold positions of high responsibility and great power in any given society, it must not blind us to the fact that in some real measure it is true of all of us. It may be that, in the final judgement of God, those who have less responsible positions in society have the greater sin, and it is not for us to presume to anticipate that final judgement. But history would have no meaning if the theory of ''the equality of guilt'' rendered us impotent to pass interim judgements, and to use them, both in order to understand history and as a means to help us to play an integral part in its movement.

Of course, we are all subject to these idolatrous pretensions. We are all conditioned by our environment and our position in society. But the greater the position the person holds, the greater his responsibility and power. The greater his personal hold of that wealth which gives him power over others irrespective of his capacity to use it rightly, the greater his temptation, and the more far-reaching the effects of his decisions over other people's lives. When all this is allied to an hereditary and class position in which from infancy the idea is inculcated that all this power, position, and wealth is his by inalienable right (almost by divine right), and he is taught to regard those who question that right as ''enemies of the human race'', the temptation to regard all this as above question is wellnigh irresistible.

But if this were all there is to be said the situation would be hopeless, and history nothing but a dog-fight. Alongside this fact of sin and its idolatrous effects we must place the fact of the ''givenness of man'', and the consequences of the whole redemptive action of God in history.

Both the Jewish nation and the Christian Church are more than mere human organisations with a place in history. In so far as they are that, the sinful men and women who compose them at any particular point in history are subject to the same temptations, and the organisations subject to the same stresses and strains, as any other historical organisations. But both are something more. They bear witness to the continuous operation of God in history. St. Stephen, standing before the same council which condemned Jesus, while denouncing them as the ''betrayers and murderers'' of Jesus, is at pains to point out that, though throughout its history the Jewish nation had been constantly rebellious, yet it was through the life of that ''Church'' that God had been continuously active in history. The very ''Church'' which condemned Jesus is the Church through which God became incarnate, and which made possible His redemptive work in the world.

In the same manner the Christian Church is more than an organisation of sinful human beings. It is the Body of Christ and the instrument by which He carries on His redemptive work to-day. If we stand to be judged for our betrayals, we are judged by the very Person whom we witness to by our life as a Church, and who through us is still active in redemption in the world. Our greatest danger of betrayal is when we seem in the eyes of the world to be most powerful, for it generally means that we have "conformed to this world". The Church's witness to Christ Jesus in the world is most penetrating when she seems to be weak and not esteemed of men—in persecution, in missions where the Christ she proclaims stands in contrast to the world about her. A difficult task confronts her whenever her work meets with some success, and her sons and daughters are called upon to "rule" in the secular world.

It is just at this point that she needs to be most insistent in holding up her crucified Lord as the Judge of the activity and life of her own children. But the point of greatest danger comes when that rule of Christian-minded persons is confronted by God working in the world. The Spirit of God is active outside the Church as well as within her, and her sons and daughters are from time to time faced with a great challenge—whether, in fact, power has so corrupted them and blinded their vision that they are incapable of accepting the sacrifices demanded by their living Lord in a changing world. They are then called on to reveal whether or not their original obedience has degenerated into idolatry, so that they are seeking to hide from God's judgement areas of life which make them comfortable in a sinful world.

The history of modern Britain is the history of this challenge of God to us. It comes most insistently not because of our failure, but because of our success. We are at least nominally a Christian country. We have, as a society, accepted a belief in the Fatherhood of God and the Christian valuation of men as children of God as the basis of our life. It is, of course, easy to show how persistently the implications of this belief have been denied in practice; but so long as society accepted Christianity and the Christian moral "standard" as the basis for its social life, they remained the criterion by which personal relationships and social action were judged. Not only so, but they served as a lever by means of which social changes were continually being made.

Because our people generally did believe that certain things about themselves and one another were true, even when it seemed inconvenient to believe them, and because they believed in God incarnate in Christ and active in redemption, the true value and dignity of persons rested upon something outside history and yet involved in it. Hence they were convicted of sin whenever they attempted to treat individuals as mere means to an end in history.

In such a society we witness the gradual growth of representative institutions to give expression to the need and demand of persons for responsibility in every sphere of life. The development of such institutions was not continuous, for there is always a tension between self-interest and the rights and duties of a man's "neighbour"; but so long as men held this belief they were bound in some measure to implement it in their social arrangements. Such freedom as we enjoy, democracy and democratic institutions, the vote, women's suffrage, educational and social welfare institutions and the implementing of the principle of self-determination in our overseas relationships, witness to the recognition of the rights and duties of the individual irrespective of his perceived value to current society. Their growth has been irregular amid the conflict between economic demands and religious belief; and the history of trade unions, as well as of factory legislation and limitations on the use of child labour, has many fearful and bloody passages. Nevertheless, that history is not complete without reference to the strength which religious values gave to their protagonists, and the way in which they sapped the resistance of those who opposed them.

The enormous advances made in our system of the administration of justice, in our treatment of criminals, in our hospitals and social services generally, would not have been possible apart from this spur and check. In face of it, the right of the working man to organise could not for long be denied, and attempts to crush the exercise of that right were defeated by causes which were not entirely economic. Those most desperately bent on opposing it found themselves confronted by a corporate conscience which they could not in the end resist.

Even the supporter of capitalism and imperialism was restrained from complete ruthlessness in his economic policy because of the conflict within himself, however much at times he tried to hide behind necessity. It was not merely hypocrisy which linked missionary zeal with empire building. It is true, no doubt, that certain chapters of the history of the growth of British imperialism are black enough, and that its growth is inexplicable apart from the economic demands which drove the capitalist to seek markets and raw materials and led him to exploit the native people of the countries he invaded. The fact remains, nevertheless, that he could neither satisfy his own conscience, nor that of his contemporaries, unless he could show another side to the picture by his missionary zeal and by his talk of imperialism as "a white man's burden" and not merely his privilege.

Indeed, it is generally true to say that these Christian beliefs acted so continuously as a check on the worst features of the capitalist system and forced modifications within it to such an extent that by-products, such as education, democratic institutions, and increased leisure, were used to justify the system itself. As a consequence Christians were sometimes blinded to its real nature, and the Church came to be regarded as a partner in a capitalist imperialist alliance, and therefore an associate in all the abuses which sprang from it.

But capitalist imperialism is, in fact, a contradiction of the Christian way of life, not only because of its economic exploitation, but because it demands for its maintenance a class system resting upon an economic foundation which is a denial of true Christian values. Sooner or later, as it develops and reaches its crisis, this is bound to become clear. The conflict between the economic demands of the system and the rights and duties of persons will inevitably become critical, and a decisive battle will remain to be fought as to which is to be paramount. Either steps must be taken to control the powers of production and distribution and the whole apparatus by which social life is organised, in order to give effect to the belief that all men are children of God and that they may not be used as mere means to a material end; or the individual must be completely subordinated to the machine, and society in general to the interests of the few who have continued to secure control of it.

In this matter I feel that a great many people have been misled by those who wish them to believe that the real danger of a "totalitarian state" comes from the Socialist. About the danger of totalitarianism under Socialism I shall have to say something later. But, at the moment, it is necessary to look more closely into the argument that this very danger of totalitarianism arises from the very nature of capitalism and is a natural by-product of it rather than alien to it in principle. In more than one country in the past monopolistic capitalism has so controlled the State, and through it the lives of the masses, that the cry "You have nothing to lose but your chains" was meaningful to millions of enslaved people. It is well to remind those who feared and were discussing this totalitarian trend in Britain before the war that they were analysing the development of capitalism in a society which had never yet had a Socialist Government in power. It is true that for two short periods between the wars the Socialists were a minority in office. But they were entirely dependent upon a hostile majority which allowed them to continue in power only so long as they did nothing to alter radically the established order. The latter continued to be administered by machinery controlled by the masters of the economic system.

Real political power in this country has always rested upon an economic foundation, now of land, now of industry and banking. The various groups who exercised that power—Whigs, Tories, Liberals, Conservatives, as the case may be—used as their tool the machinery of administration which we call the State, and used it increasingly, as the need arose, to strengthen the power concentrated in their hands.

President Woodrow Wilson in 1923 wrote of the United States: "The facts of the situation amount to this: that a comparatively small number of men control the raw materials of this country; that a comparatively small number of men largely control the water power; that the same number of men control the railroads; that by agreements handed around among themselves they control prices; and that same group of men control the larger credits of the country. The masters of the Government of the United States are the combined capitalists and manufacturers of the United States." That has been equally true of this country.

The machinery which they have increasingly used for the maintenance of that power is the State. By it they controlled the police and the armed forces, and used the latter to defeat their commercial rivals and to further their imperialist ventures. By the use of the State machine they controlled education in most of its ranges as well as the administration of relief and similar social agencies, and made them subservient to their needs. It is significant that in this country at one stage they found it necessary to control "religion", to "establish the Church" and forbid rival organisations. Little by little they gathered into their hands every agency of importance in the life of the people whenever that seemed necessary for their purpose. By means of the power of the State they enclosed the common land, drove the smallholders into manufacture, created the vast landed estates, and undermined British agriculture in the interests of the new mechanised industrialism, by which in turn those who were driven into the new towns and made cogs in a machine lost almost any semblance of freedom as persons.

It is, of course, true that this concentration of power is not a continuous process. It ebbs and flows with the needs of those who control it and with the pressure of the various agencies I have before alluded to. At one stage, for instance, the ruling class felt it necessary to forbid the formation of trade unions, and under the Combination and corresponding Acts those who attempted to form them in the teeth of the law were imprisoned, hung, deported, or driven to starve by unemployment. Later, in the face of the growing agitation, when an expanding market made it possible for them to make concessions without endangering their own power, they not only allowed their growth, but conferred a definite legal status on them. Later again, they have attempted to bring their political activities under a measure of State control.

But, again and again, trade unionism has shown itself to be a menace to the maintenance of their power. Even when the unions do not appear as an attempt to set up a rival working-class organisation which might eventually threaten their control of the State (such a state of affairs was feared by many at the time of the General Strike), they demand certain standards of life for their members. They stand in the way of reorganisations demanded from time to time by the changing methods of production and the need to produce more and more goods at lower and lower cost. On occasions they dislocate the machine by organised action at inconvenient moments. The mere existence of trade unions witnesses to the fact that men are not machines and to the rights and liberties of the individual and group against the danger of the totalitarian State.

In the decline of capitalism, therefore, we begin to witness greater and greater battles between these groups and the capitalist State of the past. The Trades Disputes Act, the compulsory separation of the Civil Service Unions from the

Trades Union Congress, the declaration of the illegality of sympathetic strikes, are all indications of this struggle in its early stages. It is our contention that, while the capitalist in this country, because of his Christian heritage, is glad to be able to grant concessions, to raise the standard of life of the workers, to grant liberty to the individual, to develop representative institutions, etc., whenever he is able to do so without endangering his privileged position and his powers of control over the lives of others, the system itself involves him in such inherent contradictions that sooner or later he is forced to declare the real value of his religious pretensions. That vital stage of development has already been reached in more than one country in our own day, and the whole world is at this moment at the parting of the ways.

In that battle Socialism stands, in general, in the Christian tradition, recognising the rights and value of the individual, desiring to free him from enslavement to the machine and to the few who control it, and recognising that, in order to do this, it is necessary to wrest the State from the domination of the few, and to use its power to secure that the means of life are in the hands of society as a whole and used for the common good. Neither the fact that Socialists are divided as to the means of effecting the change needed to ensure that the State can perform normally its proper function as the organ of the whole community, nor the fact that a major battle will come later to ensure that the control of the State is not just transferred from one tyrannical clique to another and perhaps worse one, must be allowed to blind us to the real nature of the major political struggle of our day. The centre of that struggle is a sharp conflict of convictions as to the nature and purpose of the State.

In general, I think it is true to say that the Socialist in Great Britain has envisaged the capture of the State as a necessary step towards the securing of real liberty for the individual and the group. To this end he desires as much devolution of power as possible. He has resisted Communism because he feared that the Communist tactic was likely to land him in a totalitarianism which he detests. As a Socialist he has consistently clung to a tradition which linked freedom with the right to such personal possessions as are not inimical to community life.

However valuable distributivism is as a protest against the danger of totalitarianism, it is in effect an attempt to evade this central problem of the nature and purpose of the State, for that which is to be distributed must first be wrested from those who monopolise land and the major forms of capital, and who maintain their monopoly by means of the power of the State. In fact, I think it is true to say that distributivism is an attempt to resolve the dilemma in which the Papal encyclicals placed the Roman Catholic Socialists in Great Britain through the failure of the Papacy to distinguish between the Socialism which, as in England, originated in and maintained a Christian tradition and the variety, much more prevalent on the Continent, which had become "anti-clerical" and often publicly "atheist".

But if British Socialism generally stands within that tradition of freedom, Fascism has set up its antithesis and is in a very real sense the natural development of capitalism. Sooner or later in every country capitalism is forced to face the contradictions which prevent its natural development. Confronted by the growing demand of masses of human beings to be treated as persons and not "hands", it must either allow such radical changes in the structure of society that the ownership of things no longer carries with it inordinate power over persons or declare openly that such ownership properly carries with it such power. If capitalism does the first, it capitulates to Socialism. If it does the second, then it asserts that the rights of human beings are derived from their status in society, that their duties are such as other persons assign to them, that their value is dependent upon their utility to the dominant powers in society.

Fascism in more than one country has already declared that the time has come when these inherent weaknesses must be faced, an end made to the conflict between theory and practice, and a new theory of man evolved to give justification to the new needs of society. The common man must be made completely subject to the few controllers, and all that interferes with the efficiency of the juggernaut created by them must go. "Fascism," says Mussolini, "combats the whole complex system of democratic ideology and repudiates it: it affirms the immutable, beneficial, and fruitful inequality of mankind."[1] With that conclusion the final stage of the process is reached. The State, controlled by the few, takes the place of God, and its needs become the one criterion. Every activity of man must be subordinated to it: religion becomes but a department of State and God a State puppet. To this complete idolatry human beings are to be prostituted.

Now, it would, in my opinion, be quite false to assume that the members of the ruling class in this country have ever yet, as a body, reached this stage, though a certain number of them have done so, and at times in our history they have come dangerously near to it as a body. They have been saved from it, as yet, partly by the fact that they, too, have been conditioned by a Christian tradition, partly because our island position saved us from much of the continuous turmoil which beset continental nations as the battleground of centuries of conflict, partly because the early growth in England of economic and financial imperialism gave them enormous assets upon which they could draw in order to prolong their power and absorb the first shocks of decline.

If it be argued that this whole case falls to the ground because the British capitalist, along with the rest of us, showed his detestation of Fascism by fighting it in the end, the answer surely is simple. It is that, while he naturally detested and hated its excesses and brutalities, his intense concern for his own immediate interests, and his hatred of Communism as inimical to them, led him to assist in the building up of the Fascism which in the end he was forced

[1] B. Mussolini, *The Political and Social Doctrine of Fascism*, p. 14.

to fight when he could no longer control it. Far from resisting it in Japan, Italy, Spain, and Germany in its early stages, he was prepared to make accommodation with it until he was driven by necessity to combat something which became a real danger to his own power.

Even as far back as 1920 Lloyd George, in a memorandum to the big four at Versailles, could say: "The greatest danger that I see in the present situation is that Germany may throw in her lot with Bolshevism and place her resources, her brains, her vast organising power, at the disposal of the revolutionary fanatics whose dream it is to conquer the world for Bolshevism by force of arms." That fear, not only of the armed force of Bolshevism, but of its propaganda, which they regarded in the words of Sir George Buchanan, as "dangerous and attractive in this country to those who have nothing to lose" was decisive of their early policy.

In 1927 Mr. Winston Churchill welcomed the success of Mussolini's "triumphal struggle", because by it Italy "has provided the necessary antidote to the Russian poison. Hereafter no great nation will be unprovided with an ultimate means of protection against the cancer or growth of Bolshevism".[1] Sir Arthur Balfour, a leading steel magnate, was reported in the *Sheffield Daily Telegraph*[2] as saying in 1933 "either we are to have Communism or something else. Hitler has produced Hitlerism as we see it to-day, and of the two I think it preferable." He was in favour of letting Germany rearm because "one of the greatest menaces to peace in Europe to-day is the totally unarmed condition of Germany". After Japan attacked China Mr. Amery argued in the House of Commons that nothing should be done about it. "Our whole policy in India, our whole policy in Egypt, stands condemned if we condemn Japan."[3] It was only after they had been assured by the Maffrey report of

[1] Speech in Rome. Reported in *The Times*, 21st January 1927. See *Hansard*, col. 938, 8th December 1944. [2] 24th October 1933.

[3] Speech in House of Commons, 27th February 1933. *Hansard*, col. 81.

1935 that "there is no important British interest in Abyssinia, with the exception of Lake Tsana, the waters of the Blue Nile, and certain tribal grazing rights",[1] that the Government attempted to do a deal with Italy safeguarding those rights, but acknowledging "Italian need for expansion"[2] at the expense of Abyssinia. It was this course of policy which led to the Hoare-Laval scandal and to the rape of Abyssinia by Italy.

This primary concern for the interests of those who had "something to lose" was made clear by Mr. Duncan Sandys (Mr. Churchill's son-in-law) in a speech in 1935. "Germany should be clearly asked, once her honour is satisfied, to make a categorical declaration freely renouncing all actual territorial claims and ambitions in the Colonial field. This is the one and only question which is of direct and vital interest to Great Britain and to the British Empire. If Germany once again becomes a Colonial power, not only will her interests clash with ours in that field, but she will also inevitably be drawn into rivalry with us as a naval power. Surely, then, it is the first elementary duty of British statesmanship to see to it that the great energies, ambitions and enthusiasms of the new Germany are directed into channels where they will not clash with the essential interests of Great Britain."[3]

That policy was pursued when Hitler marched into Austria; was called "peace with honour" when Czechoslovakia was betrayed; and was continued as late as 16th March 1939, when the Federation of British Industries concluded an agreement with the *Reichsgruppe Industrie* of Germany to replace "unhealthy competition" by "constructive co-operation",[4] and in July of that year, when it was stated generally in the Press that Mr. Hudson was negotiating a thousand million loan to Hitler.

[1] Speech of Mr. Eden in House of Commons, 24th February 1926. *Hansard*, col. 8.

[2] Speech of Sir Samuel Hoare in House of Commons, 11th July 1935. *Hansard*, col. 519.

[3] Speech in House of Commons, 2nd May 1935. *Hansard*, col. 597.

[4] See *The Times*, 17th March 1939.

5

THE APPEAL OF COMMUNISM

WHAT, then, is this Communism which in many quarters is feared more than Fascism?

So many books have been written on the subject that it would be impertinent for me to attempt anything like an analysis of it in the short space at my disposal. I shall not attempt, therefore, to deal with Marxism as a philosophy, but merely with the tactics for social change which the Communist Party have erected on the basis of that philosophy, and with its interpretation of history. My aim is to state the Communist case as fairly as I can, and I reserve my criticisms of it to a later stage. There are three things which I want to say by way of introduction.

1. We owe a great debt to Karl Marx for providing one indispensable key to history, and owe it no less as Christians than as sociologists. Obviously Marx, who wrote two generations or more ago, is not to be swallowed wholesale. It seems to me equally obvious, however, that he must be taken seriously if we are to arrive at any true understanding of the history of our time.

2. That, whatever criticism I may make of the Communist attitude to persons, Marxism arose partly out of an intense love for persons and a real desire to save them from intolerable injustice and age-long suffering. Marx himself began with a bias. Whatever mistakes he made, they are those of a man concerned to find a clue to history which would give hope to the workers of his day and reveal a way out of its misery to the depressed class to which they belonged.

3. Modern Communism must be approached sympathetically, for, in general, these same characteristics are to be found in many of its adherents. It is not easy to find in

modern history a parallel to the readiness for self-sacrifice and devotion to a cause shown by members of the Communist Party. They believe that the proletariat are destined to end the history of injustice and exploitation by seizing power and using it for truly social ends. Their reading of history has convinced them that the present ruling class will never relinquish power without compulsion and violence. If that seemed to be true when Karl Marx wrote, how far have events since then so changed the situation, and the people in it, that we can expect radical changes in the structure of society to take place without resort to violence?

A century has elapsed since the Communist Manifesto was published. The Britain to which Karl Marx came was a Britain in which, according to a report in 1832, little children were with their mothers "chained fast to the iron machine which knows no suffering and no weariness", and in which the report of the commission of 1842 told of "the race that lived underground like the refugees in *Les Miserables*, who lived in the sewers of Paris", and of little children who were carried on their fathers' backs and put in cradles down the coal-mines to keep the rats off their dinners.[1] In 1815, in London, relief was "seldom bestowed without the parish claiming the exclusive right of disposing at their pleasure of all the children of the persons receiving relief",[2] so that children from 7 to 11 were taken away from their homes in London and carted to be indentured till they were 21 in the mills in the north, where they worked for fourteen hours a day, including Saturdays and part-time Sundays, and when the mills stopped work were sometimes taken away in carts and turned adrift to shift for themselves. Yet the owners continuously resisted attempts to shorten hours and better conditions, because, as one of them who worked his children from 6 a.m. to 8 p.m. said at the enquiry, "Nothing is more favourable to morals than habits of early subordina-

[1] Quoted by Hammond in *The Town Labourer*, pp. 21, 28.

[2] Report of Committee on Parish Apprentices, 1815. Hammond, op. cit., p. 145 f.

tion, industry and regularity''.[1] We read in the report of 1842 of boys and girls of 8 years working down the mines as ''trappers'', or with ''girdles round their waists, crawling along on their hands and knees'', drawing the coal along the narrow passages, ''chained, belted, harnessed like dogs in a go-cart, black, saturated with wet and more than half-naked. Crawling upon their hands and feet, and dragging their heavy loads behind them, they present an appearance indescribably disgusting and unnatural''.[2] We read of chimney boys bought and sold at £8 apiece if they were small enough to do the job, and apprenticed as young as 5 years old[3]—human beings openly treated as a commodity with, like any other commodity, a market price—and that, so short a time ago, in this England, that Karl Marx was speaking to people who could remember it. We read of the creation of the great estates by the destruction of small-holdings and of the enclosure of common lands; and of the driving of the cottagers, with their hand industries, into the huge sprawling cities with their belching chimneys and back-to-back houses. It was in that world, where luxury abounded on the one side and terrible misery on the other—the England which Benjamin Disraeli described as consisting of two nations—that Karl Marx wrote his *Das Kapital.*

He could see no way out for the dispossessed by legal methods; for not only Parliament, but the whole apparatus of the State—the whole legal and civil administrative machine—was in the hands of the oppressing class. He could see no hope in religion, for the bishops as often as not voted against any reforms, and the clergy supported the squire and the magistracy. The only hope lay in the forcible overthrow of the system by the masses themselves.

Was this possible? Not at that time, for the masses were ignorant, disunited, and slave-minded.

Was it possible that the demands of the system itself would

[1] Hammond, op. cit., p. 163.

[2] Children's Employment Commission, First Report, Mines, 1842. Hammond, op. cit., p. 173 f.

[3] House of Lords Report, 1818. Hammond, op. cit., p. 178 f.

educate the masses, make them conscious of their unity, and eventually create a situation in which the forcible overthrow of the exploiters would be possible?

It is with such thoughts that Marx begins his study of history. He sees that in every social system changes are continually going on in the material forces of production. Sooner or later new methods of production come into conflict with the old property relations, and a revolutionary situation is reached in which a new group comes into power. Looking at the contemporary situation he prophesied that the changing methods of production would necessitate the education of the workers as the need for skilled hands increased, and that the very organisation of their work would make it possible for them to know one another better and to consolidate their forces in a common cause. As time went on, and new methods of production developed, a situation would arise where, under the existing property relationships, there would be a huge accumulation of goods, and still greater potential powers of production, which were incapable of being fully exploited. This would lead to unemployment and want—in fact, starvation in the midst of plenty. That might mean merely increased suffering and misery for the masses. But it need not mean that. It is in the nature of history—a dialectical process—for the ruling class, in its progression and decline, to create its antithesis, its own opposition. "Capitalism breeds in its womb the seeds of its own destruction."

In the particular system with which Marx was confronted that opposition was no longer a different minority class of property-owners, but the proletariat—the majority—those who have all along been enslaved, but at last are educated, organised, and capable of seizing power and ruling.

A revolution is only possible when a whole series of factors coincide. At that moment it is the historic role of the working class to seize power; only so can their slavery and misery be ended. But they cannot of themselves produce a revolutionary situation. The necessary conditions for a successful revolution are not only a revolutionising of the consciousness of the new class—an ideological revolution in the class that is to serve as the grave-digger of the old society—but a breakdown of the forces of production and distribution, and a general economic crisis in which the ruling class is divided against itself and incapable of ruling. "The fundamental law of revolution," says Lenin later, "confirmed by all revolutions, and particularly by the three Russian ones of the twentieth century, is as follows. It is not sufficient for the revolution that the exploited and oppressed masses understand the impossibility of living in the old way, and demand changes; for the revolution it is necessary that the exploiters should not be able to rule as of old. Only when the masses do not want the old régime, and when the rulers are unable to govern as of old, then only can the revolution succeed. This truth may be expressed in other words: revolution is impossible without an all-national crisis, affecting both the exploited and the exploiters."[1]

But long before that situation is reached social discontent grows. Marx believed that during that period there would be some who could see farther than the others, "new thinkers and prophets who in an apparently strange dialect, and in accordance with their temperament, knowledge, and character attempt to interpret the crisis". This is the early role of the Communist Party. If the ruling class at this stage, before the revolution, are forced to grant certain concessions in order to ward off revolution, the Communist Party must lead the workers to see their significance as evidence of the weakness of the system, and use every opportunity to hasten the inevitable crisis, and to widen the gap rather than to assist in closing it.

While pursuing these tactics on the economic level, they must seek to capture the machinery of the State on the political level. Capitalist democracy is a sham. Even if the workers obtained a majority at the polls, and sought to

[1] Lenin, *Infantile Sickness of "Leftism" in Communism*. Quoted by S. Hook, *Towards the Understanding of Karl Marx*, p. 233.

transform capitalism by peaceful means, the capitalist would use his economic power to render their efforts futile, and even resort to force to overthrow them. But political effort can be used to demonstrate to the workers the futility of peaceful methods and is for that reason valuable. When the situation has developed sufficiently, and the revolutionary frame of mind of the workers coincides with the external pressure on them by the inability of the system to satisfy their needs, a conflict will ensue in which a definite break with the old society is possible. The workers must then assume the offensive, forcibly break the will of the enemy, and impose on him acceptance of the ends for which the workers fight. Only determined use of force can seize power and hold it. "A revolutionary class," says Trotsky, "which has conquered power with arms in its hands, is bound to, and will, suppress, rifle in hand, all attempts to tear power out of its hands. Where it has against it a hostile army, it will oppose to it its own army. Where it is confronted with armed conspiracy, attempts at murder or rising, it will hurl at the heads of its enemy an unsparing penalty."

Having thus captured the State the Communist proposes to consolidate his position. He aims, through the socialisation of the means of production, to destroy the capitalist State and to create a new classless State, free and democratic. But in the transition period there is to be a dictatorship of the working class. To quote Max Beer, " 'The transition' from Capitalism to Socialism will have as its political organ the revolutionary dictatorship of the proletariat. It will use its political supremacy to wrest by degrees all capital from the bourgeoisie, to centralise all instruments of production in the hands of the State (i.e. of the proletariat organised as the ruling class) and to increase the total productive forces as rapidly as possible."[1]

This is in reality a dictatorship on behalf of the working class exercised by the Communist Party. Lenin says that "during a revolution—a revolution which has aroused the

[1] Max Beer, *History of British Socialism*, Vol. II, p. 212.

masses, the majority of the workers and peasants—only that power can be stable which avowedly and unconditionally rests upon the majority of the population''.

If, then, this dictatorship is to be effective, the Communist Party must contain the *élite* of the working class, who through all the period of preparation have gained the confidence of the working class, and who have been so educated and disciplined that they can become its vital instrument. ''Without a party of iron,'' says Lenin, ''tempered to the art of conflict, and enjoying the confidence of all the honest elements of the working class, knowing how to observe and to influence the spirit of the masses, such a conflict as ours cannot be conducted.''

The building up of this organ is an integral part of the Communist method. A good deal of their propaganda, if not most of it, is directed towards this separation from the masses of the most intelligent, class-conscious, and energetic of the workers, and the training and disciplining of them for their immediate work and the more difficult tasks which lie ahead. Behind the Charter campaign, the Minority movement, and such-like efforts between the wars, this policy could be seen at work in Britain. They were attempts to deal with live issues and real working-class problems in such a way as to gain the respect of the working class for Communist Party leadership, and to show up the opportunism of rival leadership. ''I support Henderson by my vote as a rope supports a man who is being hanged,'' said Lenin.

''As the Civil War becomes more fierce, the Communist Party can only accomplish its task by being highly centralised. Its discipline must be of iron, and almost military in character; it must be ruled by a central committee with wide powers.'' Open discussion is allowed within the party; but once a decision is arrived at no dissent is allowed. The party line must be followed in its entirety.

As a result of this dictatorship, resting on the good will of the workers, industry, the banks, the means of distribution, etc., will be taken over and run by the State, the workers educated in the new ideas, and weaned from the false ideology of the old system, and the minds of men made ready for the new social relationship.

The State will wither away when it has fulfilled its function. To quote Lenin again: "When the people have become accustomed to observe the fundamental principle of social life, and their labour is so productive that they will voluntarily work according to their abilities, there will then be no need for any exact calculation by society of the quantity of the products to be distributed to each of its members; each will take freely according to his needs."

Now, I am not primarily concerned to criticise this avowed aim of Communism. There is nothing anti-Christian in it; indeed, parallels to it can be found in both the Old and the New Testaments, though the latter explicitly, and the former implicitly, puts such an objective beyond history—as, indeed, in a curious way, the Marxian does as well. But in so far as it can be viewed historically as an objective within history, it posits an optimistic view of some men, and a completely pessimistic view of others, which is contrary both to human experience and to Christian theory. At the moment, however, I am much more concerned about the tactics by which it is proposed to reach such an end.

First, let us clear away some of the false arguments used against those tactics by those who in general support capitalist imperialism. They argue that dictatorship is wrong in principle, even if it ever attains its avowed aim of freedom; yet they themselves talk glibly of "the white man's burden" and the "tutelage of subject races", and claim that they only use force to assert their sovereignty in a transitional period. What is the fundamental distinction between the imperialist method of "ruling subject nations for their good" and the Communist dictatorship? Is it merely that they assume that they can be trusted to exercise such power and relinquish it at will, and that the Communist cannot?

They say that, even if the Communist objective is a good one, some human beings have no right to inflict suffering on others in order to attain it; that the individual person is sacred; and that one group of human beings has no right to short-circuit suffering by inflicting suffering on numberless innocent men, women, and children; that the end, in short, does not justify the means. Yet these same people argue that it was necessary to bombard mercilessly, and wipe out, open towns in war; and claimed, without vigorous protest by the religious organisations as a whole, that it was right to drop atom bombs on Nagasaki and Hiroshima, because it would shorten the war and in the end save lives. When the Dean of Chichester stated that "Communism builds its Utopia on the dead bodies of those who have contributed to it", the Communist replies that that is surely better than to maintain an evil system on the dead bodies and living corpses of whose who are enslaved by it.

The Communist, that is to say, looks backwards, and sees through the long centuries misery and poverty existing alongside of comparative luxury. Looking forward, he sees this same misery of millions of human beings stretching far ahead. Is there no way out? He begins by an examination of the situation in which he finds himself, and the history which gave it birth, not as an intellectual exercise, but in order to try to discover some way by which he can give hope of release to the suffering masses and help them out of their condition. Taking the totality of human beings concerned, he comes to the conclusion that, by working with the forces of history, he can give the masses now, who have been deprived of real personal life, a consciousness of genuine value by relating them to a class with an historic destiny, and so making them partners in an enterprise which will finally bring freedom and justice to mankind. He also holds that, in their totality, the numbers sacrificed to that end are as nothing compared with the continuous destruction of persons, and actual denial of any real value and dignity to them, if this pageant of hell is allowed to continue through the ages ahead.

Sidney Hook, in his book *Towards the Understanding of*

Karl Marx,[1] says: "To judge anything *only* by its cost is to condemn everything ever undertaken and carried to completion in this imperfect world. Hardly a major good has come down from the past, from the discovery of fire and speech to the latest development of scientific technique, for which human beings have not paid a price in blood and tears. Both logic and morality demand, however, that before we reject a proposal because of its cost we consider the cost of rejecting it for any of the available alternatives. The Marxist contention is that the costs of social revolution are far less than the costs of the chronic evils of poverty, unemployment, moral degradation, and war, which are immanent in capitalism; that the ultimate issue and choice is between imperialistic war, which promises nothing but the destruction of all culture, yes, of the human race itself, and an international revolution which promises a new era in world history."

It is evident that Marx had in mind this continuous suffering of the working class when he described what he believed would be the development of the system of his day. "All methods for raising the social productiveness of labour are effected at the cost of the individual labourer; all means for the development of production transform themselves into means of dominating and exploiting the producer. They mutilate him into a fragment of a man; they degrade him to the level of an appendage to a machine. Every remnant of charm in his work is destroyed and transformed into a loathsome toil; he is separated from the intellectual possibilities of the labour process in the same degree that science, as an independent agency, becomes part of it; they distort the conditions under which he works, and subject him as he labours to a despotism made the more hateful by its meanness. They transform his life time into working time, and his wife and child are dragged beneath the wheels of the Juggernaut of Capital. . . . Accumulation of wealth, at one end of the pole, is at the same time accumulation of

[1] ibid., p. 248.

misery, agonised toil, slavery, ignorance, brutality, mental degradation at the opposite pole."

Now, the comfortable arm-chair critic can no doubt point out that that description of a particular period of growth of industrialism in England is one-sided, and that anyway much has happened since which falsifies it as a prophecy. Even, however, if Marx was wrong because he could not anticipate perfectly the future development of capitalist imperialism and its effects in this country, is he so wrong if we take the international view which was so continuously in his mind? Is there anything worse in human history than Guernica, Belsen, Buchenwald, and Hiroshima? Has human life ever been held as cheaply as in our own day? Are these things due merely to the fact that there are a few bad people in the world, and have they no relationship to the breakdown of the same world economy which Marx analysed? Apart from the fact of the closely knit and interrelated international economy of the modern world, which imposes a real responsibility on all nations for the economic breakdown in any part, is it not true that these happenings show us that there is no level of bestiality to which human beings are not capable of sinking when driven by fear, or love of power, or sheer material necessity, or a combination of all three—driven, that is, by some need which becomes for them absolute?

Have we in this country suddenly become better people, who now merely look back on these things as part of a past of which we are ashamed? Or is it just possible that they have been changed because we discovered new methods of exploitation overseas, and that the freedom and better conditions of life of the British worker and the parallel increase in comfort and luxury of the owning class have been at the expense of the Indians in the mills of Bombay, the Chinese coolies, and the Kaffirs of Johannesburg? Is it true that we are better than other men? Or is it more likely that we have been saved by our comparatively secure and prosperous condition from that very fear and want which have been so

H

fatal to others? If, between the two wars, with all our potential productive powers and our actual wealth, we acquiesced in Britain in millions of people being unemployed and their wives and families being underfed, badly housed, and deprived of so much of their freedom, what would we do if our security were really threatened and our whole economy dislocated? We should do well to remember the derelict areas of Durham and South Wales, the deserted shipyards of Jarrow and the hunger-marchers, in a rich country. "If they do these things in the green tree, what shall be done in the dry?"

But, whatever we may think about it, the Communist does honestly hold that there is no length to which the ruling class will not go in order to maintain its power, that "the history of all hitherto existing society is the history of class struggles",[1] and that only in the pursuance of these struggles can the working class be freed from fear, injustice, and exploitation. He is not inhibited by any *a priori* assumptions about human nature, for, as Trotsky said, he is "not concerned with the Kantian, Priestley and vegetarian Quaker prattle about the sacredness of human life. To make the individual sacred we must destroy the social order which crucifies him, and this problem can only be solved by blood and iron."

Believing all this, his tactics are clear and logical.

1. Men everywhere demand some explanation of the bewildering facts of life. They are worried by the situation which faces them and live in constant fear of the future. The Marxian conception and analysis of history may not give a complete answer to all their problems, but it does seem to answer the more pressing ones. They want to know why, with all the modern inventions and the powers of production at the disposal of society to-day, there is "starvation in the midst of plenty"; why they are unemployed when there is so much that needs to be done; why they are living in hovels when there is so much money available and brick-

[1] *Manifesto of the Communist Party*, p. 10.

layers unemployed. These and other pressing problems seem to them to require a clear answer. The Communist comes with a clear answer which not only seems reasonable, but which is supported by a philosophy of life and a guide to the future. He claims that this arises from his study of history. It does, in fact, explain satisfactorily most of the obvious facts of which his hearers are aware, and holds out a hope of deliverance.

2. Masses of people suffering deprivation of all sorts feel that they are nonentities and do not count as persons, in spite of the Christian assertion to the contrary. To a greater or less degree they feel themselves at certain periods to be pawns in a game, and in the grip of a machine which is destroying them and their children, and over which they have no control. This feeling is devastating. The teaching of the class nature of society, and of the resulting class struggle, not only makes clear to them the cause of their situation, but makes them feel that they are capable of playing a real part as persons in a growing historical movement. It answers to their sense of the dramatic; they can understand its symbols; they become aware that they are important and matter, because they now become integrated in a movement in which they can play a real part. It succeeds in restoring to others a feeling of self-respect.

3. They need desperately to find a purpose in which they can not only play an intelligent part, but in which their sufferings are no longer inflicted upon them from without, but voluntarily accepted and explicable in terms of good. They are made to feel that here is such a purpose to which they can give themselves, and which holds out the promise of new life for them and their children. They are not merely wanted; they are now necessary as the agents of a social change which is in line with the whole process of history. They are the proletarians, the masters of the future, in the van of progress, called to submit to order and discipline by a society of which they are an integral and vital unit.

The Communist, therefore, has confronted modern society

with a genuine issue, and that issue must be faced. However much we may disagree with his analysis or attempt to minimise the decisive character of "economic determinism" as merely one factor among many, we must reckon with the facts to which he calls attention. All over Europe a social order through which we are passing, whatever its differences in different countries, has produced, visible to all who have eyes to see, a profound class division. The result is struggle between those who live as the result of the ownership of things, their distribution and exchange, and those whose only source of livelihood is the precarious one of the sale of their labour power.

Now, I know that it is not all as simple as that; that there is a large middle class; that all sorts of other factors have to be taken into account in order to explain the period of clash and war through which we are passing. But when all these factors have been taken into account the revolutions in Russia, Italy, Germany, Spain and elsewhere before the war, the war itself, the preparations for further battles now assuming gigantic proportions in Europe, together with the drawing of the smaller nations on the frontiers of Russia into one group, the battles about the Marshall plan, the breakdown of Government in France in 1947—none of these things can be understood apart from this concern for "bread", for a guaranteed means of livelihood, and the fear of further material deprivation. They are unintelligible, in short, apart from a struggle about things, in which the ideas of people as to how they are to be secured and distributed have so close a relationship to the place they find themselves in the economy of things, that they are increasingly drawn to take sides by that interest. The fact that this is so often only a sub-conscious motive, and that they are not aware of the force which directs them in this matter of taking sides, only gives weight to the fact of its compulsion. However great the number of people in any country who do not take an active part in this struggle, they are unorganised and defenceless for the very reason that they want only to be left alone.

But on either side of them stand groups conscious of the ends they seek, organised, active, and determined to achieve those ends. Sooner or later those who wish to stand neutral are drawn into that struggle for bread and power, because as human beings they cannot contract out of it and live.

On the one hand we see a group holding on to power, to the maintenance of the privileged position which the possession of things and power gives them, making endless adjustments, but seeing nothing radically wrong with the system they maintain, and fearful of change. On the other there is a group, convinced that they alone have the key to the solution, actively engaged in exposing the inequalities and injustice of that system, concerned with hastening what they believe to be the inevitable breakdown of that social order, and doing all in their power to build up the new life within its womb which will in course of time break out and redeem the world.

Now, it is obviously absurd to refuse to take seriously this whole Communist analysis and tactics merely on the ground that because he has deliberately rejected a belief in God the Communist has a very incomplete understanding of man, his purpose and destiny. It is no use saying he has a totally inadequate picture of man—that he is not just like that. The fact is (and we have abundant illustrations of it in our own time) that men do get like that, and act like that in certain situations, and that those situations are present in more places than one in Europe to-day.

It is no use saying that Marx has left out of consideration important factors in his analysis of the situation, if, in fact, he has produced a working analysis upon which men increasingly and in large areas to-day are prepared to act.

Is it, then, legitimate to take the line which Alexander Miller in his book *The Christian Significance of Karl Marx* sets down as a summary of that taken by John Macmurray in *Creative Society*? "Marxism is busy about the actual carrying into effect of the will of God, but will not expressly acknowledge Him. Official Christianity is like the son in the

Gospel who said 'I go' and went not; while Communism is like the other son who said 'I go not', but went.''[1] In effect his whole system leads to ''the equation of the Kingdom of God of the New Testament with the classless society of the Marxist scheme'', and to ''the proletariat as the instrument of the change'' from this society to that. ''. . . There is no hope of a change for the better except by revolution, and at that very hour the revolution comes the inner contradictions of capitalism work themselves out, and under the leadership of the Communist Party the proletariat (the contemporary Son of Man) gives the last push to the ill-balanced structure, and the whole society topples to come right side up—in the new classless society. The proletariat is Messiah, the agent of the purposes of history or of the purposes of God, which, on this view, are one and the same thing.''[2]

A fair number of people in this country to-day start from some such idea as that outlined by William Temple in *Nature, Man and God.* ''If materialism,'' he writes, ''once becomes dialectical, it is doomed as materialism; its own dialectic will transform it into theism.''[3] They argue, therefore, that the Communist rejection of theism does not invalidate either his analysis of that area of life with which he is concerned or his tactics for achieving his end. They find it possible to join the Communist Party, and hope that in time they will convince its members of the incompleteness of their outlook, and, as it were, introduce the Communist to God without altering his analysis and tactics materially. Without entering into the much-disputed question of this equation of the Kingdom of God with the creation by man within history of a classless society, this attitude means the acceptance of the Communist tactics.

I do not believe that the fact that capitalist imperialists have tended to treat persons as means to their ends justifies those who subscribe to the Christian view of man in doing

[1] ibid., p. 73.
[2] ibid., p. 80.
[3] ibid., p. 490.

the same thing. In fact, as I have already pointed out, our ability to convict those who do so as sinful has been one of our main levers for social change. From time to time some of my Christian friends have in desperation joined the Communist Party. None of them have remained there long. Very soon they found themselves being forced either to give up their belief in God as revealed by Jesus Christ, or to leave a party which committed them to a certain attitude to persons and to values which conflicted with that belief. They were willing to cut themselves off from the Church, but not to deny God.

The best and most thoughtful Communists recognise that real belief in God is a determinant of action; and, to my knowledge, the party has at times refused to accept as party members those whose beliefs seemed to them likely to conflict in this way. Belief in God as revealed by Jesus Christ does commit the Christian to a particular attitude to persons, and to certain values which condition conduct; in fact, to a unity of thought and action which cannot be separated. The Communist understands this. He has rejected the Christian God, because to accept God would be to make it impossible for him to act towards persons in the way that he deems necessary in order to achieve his end. He recognises also that that belief would entail the acceptance of values which would invalidate much of his analysis of history and current society.

Because he understands this he has built up a complete system of thought and action, and he demands the acceptance of this system as a whole. To argue that thought and action can be separated is to misunderstand completely the fundamental tenet of Marxism that the relationship between theory and practice is so close that the one can have no validity without the other. Marx wrote "to understand the world is to be able to change it", and he claimed to understand it. On that claim his whole analysis and conclusion is based. To "introduce him to God" would be to introduce him to a new set of values which would make it impossible for him to use persons as mere means to an end in which they are not included. To alter his conception of the nature and origin of life, and consequently of man, would be to involve him in the vital questions of sin, forgiveness, and the inescapable demand made upon him by his enemies. The Communist is so convinced of this unity of theory and practice that he will allow no deviation in theory even in those who find it possible to subscribe to his practice at any given time. His opportunism leads him at one moment to allow a few Christians to join the party, and at another to refuse them, but he retains the right to purge them at any moment that they become dangerous. In fact, his understanding of the world leads him to certain conclusions as to the end he seeks; and those ends are then, as it were, reflected back and become completely determinative of his tactics for reaching it. Everything is subordinated to his objective. All his values are so conditioned. It is this fact which is reflected in his terminology and which makes discussion difficult. Words mean different things to the two sides. By this I mean much more than the confusion about words like "social democracy". I refer to freedom, justice, and truth, which all become relative to ends in which freedom, justice, and truth are supposed to be included, and to the means by which they are to be achieved. Proletarian justice, the Communist would say, is the nearest approach to justice possible to-day, until the advent of a classless society makes it possible to drop the qualification "proletarian". That which helps to expose the fundamental capitalist lie is truth. The words have a meaning only in their context.

But, however true or false all this may be, we must still face realistically those facts with which the Communist confronts us. Marx confessedly analysed the world as he saw it, and its history within time; it is a world of sinful men. His follower to-day also sees a world in which man is enslaved by material things to such an extent that he can prophesy fairly accurately the course of social development and prepare plans to take advantage of it. He says in effect:

"This is what is going to happen, if those laws which I believe determine the growth of society work logically through to their natural end." We can, if we like, translate that into Christian language and say: "This is the situation which sin rots into, if left to work itself out." Marx claimed that he can save men from it, and his influence has inspired numberless men and women in all countries to very real sacrifices to that end. But that does not justify their methods, however much it may lead us to admire many of them as persons.

Under a Communist dictatorship, in spite of all the attempts to disguise it as a dictatorship established on behalf of the masses and supported by their good will, it still remains true that it is a class dictatorship. Experience has shown that though the Communist Party may use democratic methods—in the old-fashioned meaning of that word—during the early stages of their rise to power in any country, once they have seized power that power is exercised by a group who surround themselves with all the appurtenances of a power group and with the means of maintaining it by force. By systematic purges they see to it that no rival leadership or threat to their oligarchy arises, and soon constitute a real class in their turn, a class which grows to love power and all that power brings with it. On any understanding of man—Marxian or Christian—there is no guarantee that such people will ever relinquish that power without another violent revolution, for it is in its nature totalitarian and forbids the building up of opposition. The belief on the part of the Communist that it will abdicate in due course is baseless. Our reading of history leads us to the conclusion that sinful man, at no point in history, is free from the love of power and the desire to dominate others, and that this pride is completely determinative when he reaches the idolatrous conclusion that there is no overarching criterion by which he judges and is judged.

The attempt of Communists therefore to justify the sacrifices involved in their revolutionary procedure, and the complete ruthlessness with which they are prepared to liquidate all opposition on the ground that the end justifies the means, would fall to the ground even if we were prepared to accept their theory.

But that does not necessarily invalidate their analysis of the present economic and social situation. The class struggle may still go the way they envisage, particularly in those areas where the class divisions are most apparent, the exploitations most keenly felt, and the fear of the future most dominant.

If it does go that way, the Christian will, there as everywhere, have a duty to enter, to preach the Gospel of Jesus Christ; to help groups struggling with the problems of bread and human relationships, and individuals as they wrestle with the problems of sin and death; to offer, as always and everywhere, the means of grace, the forgiveness of sins and the life everlasting. But that demand on the Christian for fidelity to the Christian Evangel does not absolve us or others of good will from the duty of facing the problems in which we are involved by the very fact that we are part of a society and are members one of another.

The continuing crises, and the war itself, have revealed the judgement of God upon ways of life contrary to the proper nature of man as God meant him to be. The attempt to build a self-sufficient humanist society has failed, and that failure is shown in a progressive disrespect for human personality all over the world and in every sphere of life. However much men may disagree with the rights and wrongs of Communism, most people would agree that it arises only where there is chronic injustice and human suffering. That injustice and suffering is evident all over the world to-day. No nation or people can contract out of responsibility for it. All, sooner or later, become involved in the consequences of it. God meant that to be so because we are members one of another.

"Reasoning from the hopeless sinfulness of man," wrote N. Berdiaeff in an article published in *Christendom* some time before the war, "it is often argued that all effort to improve the social order or the social relations of men is useless. To create a better life is, after all, impossible. There remains only the way of personal conflict with sin and personal improvement. This is a denial of the fact that society is a reality, a special degree of reality different from the personal life of men, although connected with it. Society exists; it is constantly changing its structure for better or for worse. Social activity is constantly going on, producing countless results for individual lives. Christians cannot accept the viewpoint that someone else must always carry on social activity, must reform society. It is a great evil that the initiative in social creativity is constantly slipping from the hands of Christians, that they always act too late. It would be stupid to assert that the capitalist system cannot be changed and replaced by some better order, merely on account of the sinfulness of human nature. In principle it is essential that economic and international life be subject to spiritual and moral elements; this life must be deprived of its godless autonomy. With this there must go a new social organisation of human society. Economic and international relations, if not subject to some higher religious unity, lead to a war of all against all, as we are witnessing. It is sin which makes so essential the new social organisation of mankind on a spiritual basis. The arguments of man's fallen state, used against the social reformation of society and against social creativity, too often sound like hypocritical defence of the existing order. The argumentation merely reveals its own sinfulness. The fact of sinfulness does not mean that struggle against sin is needless. This is just as true for social as for individual life. The exploitation of man by man, or of class by class, is a product of sin, and with this sin we are called to battle. The assertion is false that Christian morals are applicable only to personal life and not to that of society or of the nation. Christianity cannot permit such a division of the unity of life. Man cannot be a good Christian, realising the Gospel principles in his personal life, and be a poor Christian, unjust and cruel, tyrannical or violent in social life, in international politics, as the proprietor of a business, as a state official or as a member of society. The man who in his private life is seeking to be perfect as his Father in Heaven is perfect, seeking the Kingdom of God, cannot, in social relations, support exploitation, oppression or predatory war. Such a sort of double-entry book-keeping is insupportable to the Christian consciousness. Such an attitude has compromised Christianity and caused many to fall away. Personal enlightenment necessarily leads to social change. Christianity in personal life is unrealisable without a Christian attitude towards others, without regard to life in the full in all its aspects. Social evil in a given form, slavery, for example, may be abolished by social reform or revolution. It would have been hopeless to wait for the moral perfection of men and their final victory over sin, to abolish slavery. The same may be said of the slavery connected with the capitalist order, the slavery of workers compelled to sell their toil as merchandise. Egoism, of class or nation, will be overcome not alone by struggle against sin, but by organising a society in which there will be neither classes in the sense of the present capitalist order nor isolated sovereign states. Moved to protest against all class struggle as incompatible with the Christian attitude, we may easily become partisans on the side of the hidden, unnoticed conflict of the ruling class, as opposed to the very evident struggle of the oppressed. Thus we would accept the greater, instead of the lesser, of two evils. In a sin-ridden world conflict is inevitable, and our concern must be to choose that which will, in principle, lessen dissension and oppression in the world. The right way to eliminate the class struggle, by which the world is torn, is to eliminate classes.''

If this is true, it is surely our duty to examine ourselves and our own immediate situation to see if there is any way by which we—that is, you and I and the British people generally—can revolutionise our own social life in such a way as to root out the more obvious injustices, iron out the most glaring inequalities and in fact produce a social order which contains at least that good for which the Communist stands, without resort to a violent revolution, and without sacrificing those values inherent in our own Christian tradition. We must do this not merely to save our own skins, or with any idea that we can maintain a Christian pocket in isolation in a heathen world torn asunder by violence, but because it is the right and proper thing to do so as our particular contribution to those struggling in less advantageous circumstances. That this means accepting real sacrifices is obvious—but that is the cost of sin, our own and that of others. Suffering is only tolerable and redemptive when it is freely accepted. The alternative is its mere sterile imposition.

At this point, when we turn to consider our particular situation in Great Britain, I think it is worth while to look at certain exceptions which Marx makes to his general rules about revolutions. In a speech in 1872 at Amsterdam he said: "Some day the workers must conquer political supremacy in order to establish the new organisation of labour; they must overthrow the old political system whereby the old institutions are sustained. If they fail to do this they will suffer the fate of the early Christians, who neglected to overthrow the old system, and who, for that reason, never had a kingdom in this world. Of course, I must not be supposed to imply that the means to this end will be everywhere the same. We know that special regard must be paid to the institutions, customs, and traditions of various lands; and we do not deny that there are certain countries, such as the United States and England, in which the workers may hope to secure their ends by peaceful means."[1]

Later, in 1886, Engels, in his preface to the first English translation of *Das Kapital*, refers to Marx, "whose whole theory is the result of a life-long study of the economic history and condition of England, and whom that study led to the conclusion that, at least in Europe, England is the only country where the inevitable social revolution might be effected entirely by peaceful and legal means". He comments

[1] Cf. G. Steckloff, *History of the First International*, p. 240.

that "he [Marx] certainly never forgot to add that he hardly expected the English ruling classes to submit, without a 'pro-slavery rebellion', to this peaceful and legal revolution".[1]

Lenin, in 1917, attempts to prove that this is no longer true. He writes ". . . he [Marx] confines his conclusions [about violent revolution] to the Continent. This was natural in 1871, when England was still the pattern of a purely capitalist country, without a military machine and, in large measure, without a bureaucracy. . . . To-day in 1917, in the epoch of the first great imperialist war, this distinction of Marx becomes unreal."[2]

Now, I do not think that this is sufficient to make us accept at its face value the statement of many members of the Communist Party in this country to-day, that they believe that they can secure their ends by peaceful and legal means. It is necessary for them thus to appear to be democratic in their methods—in the traditional sense of the word—in order to carry out their tactics of infiltration. Recent events in Czechoslovakia, where a little while ago the Communists were arguing that democratic methods were being employed to bring about a social revolution, force one to the conclusion that, once these tactics have accomplished their purpose of persuading a sufficient number of people to accept their leadership, believing it to be democratic in character, Communists resort to their traditional tactics of suppressing the liberties of those who have helped them to power, and the use of force to banish all criticism and enthrone a dictatorship. But the fact that the Communists have, from time to time, stated that the position in Great Britain was a peculiar one leads us to consider whether that is still true in our own day after the impact of the second world war.

It is of interest now to recall a tableau which I witnessed

[1] Edn. of 1938, p. xiv.
[2] *State and Revolution* (1919), p. 40. Quoted by S. Hook, op. cit., p. 245 f.

in, I think, 1926, in the Poplar Town Hall. It was staged by the Communist Party, and depicted the various nations of the world in their struggles for freedom. Soviet Russia stood beckoning, and one after another the nations rose and joined her. I remember that I was struck by the fact that it was only after China, Spain, Germany, France, Italy, and, I believe, America, that the girl representing Britain rose from a deep sleep and joined the rest with a shrug of her shoulders, as though to say: "I suppose I might as well."

6

THE SPIRITUAL TRADITION OF THE LABOUR MOVEMENT

ON the continent of Europe, down to September 1939, two great revolutionary forces faced one another in bitter antagonism—the Fascist dictatorship supreme in Italy, Germany, and Spain, and the Communist one in the Soviet Union. There was no possibility of compromise between them, and both realised that they were engaged in a life and death struggle to which all their energies were to be directed and their tactics subordinated.

Dictatorship, by definition, means that the great mass of the people have very little to say in the direction of affairs. While a certain number may manage to maintain some sort of neutrality, the majority are forced into an alignment with those in power, who have at their disposal not only the means of their immediate livelihood, together with the whole apparatus by which the public mind is informed and educated, but a military and police force ready and willing to search for and to suppress ruthlessly any attempt at deviation. Both dictatorships have, in fact, always declared that they were in this manner able to condition the minds of the masses to their purpose.

It is true that, sooner or later, because of certain fundamental contradictions to basic human laws, opposition arises both from within and without which destroys dictatorships; but those contradictions take time to become apparent, and the opposition may take decades to make itself strong enough to take effective action. In the meantime it is a comparatively small number of people who decide the policy, and direct the strategy, to which the mass of the people are subject. This means that a complete change of tactics, amounting almost to a *volte-face* which seems to carry a whole nation with it, is possible under a dictatorship to the bewilderment of a liberal democratic régime.

In order to understand the Russian-German pact of 1939 it is necessary to bear in mind this ability on the part of a dictatorship to remain true to a purpose, and yet make a quick "about turn" order which is instantly obeyed without criticism by their people. It is absurd to suggest that the pact revealed how much Communism and Fascism had in common. It is true that they are in agreement in their ruthless use of persons to their respective ends. It is the nature of all dictatorships to treat human beings in this way; to suppress at any cost opposition to the ends they seek; and to subordinate all tactics to those ends. But Fascism and Communism have diametrically opposed conceptions of the origin and nature of life, of the nation, society, State, and, perhaps most clearly, of the ultimate purpose of history and the destiny of man.

Both Hitler and Mussolini gave abundant proof at their meetings that they regarded Bolshevism as their real enemy and that they had no hope of attaining their ends until it had been completely destroyed, while the fear and hatred of Fascism is writ large in the whole history of the struggle within the Soviet Union. It is by reference to the pattern of that life and death struggle between these two mighty antagonists, who had consolidated their particular positions in their respective spheres, that we must try to understand the pre war diplomatic moves.

The great mass of the British people instinctively disliked both; but of the two they regarded Fascism as the greater evil. Against that they could at almost any period have been led to declare war; but no one could have persuaded them to do so against Communism, not merely because it was farther off and did not menace their economic interests in the same way, but because they had some sympathy with its aims and the situation in which it arose as a protest against tyranny, and because they hoped that something good would come of it.

On the other hand, the real rulers of this country, and the Government which expressed their feelings, did, I believe, regard Communism as the greater menace. While they did not want war for many reasons, among which must be included the knowledge that it would result in a further weakening of their power to control events and continue their rule, they were really concerned to see that, if war did come, it should not end with a still further strengthening of the power and influence of Communism.

Through the maze of diplomatic moves in the decade before the war there can be seen clearly on the part of our rulers four principles at work directing them and their strategy:

1. That a *modus vivendi* must be found with Fascism.
2. That that must be found without danger to our own economic interests as an imperial and colonial Power.
3. That a strong Germany was necessary as a bulwark against Communism.
4. That, if Fascism must spread, it should spread east and not west.

It is difficult to avoid the conclusion that their hope was that ultimately Germany would find herself involved in a war with the Soviet Union, which would end by a complete domination of Europe by Britain and France. That, at any rate, was the situation as seen by both Russia and Germany. The Soviet Union believed that if war broke out the western powers would stand on the west wall of Germany, leave them to bear the real onslaught of Fascism, and enter in as victors when both antagonists were too weak to resist. Germany, on the other hand, was not prepared to go to war with powerful enemies on either side of her. Therefore it suited the two of them, and was consistent with their philosophy, to make a bargain with one another. Hitler hoped to secure his eastern frontier for a time and to get some needed war materials, and Russia to assume the role which she was convinced we had reserved for ourselves, and at the same time to strengthen her dangerous western flank. Both knew only too well that the struggle between them had merely been postponed.

The war, when it came, took the course which the Soviet Union had anticipated. We stood at first on the west wall impotent, while Germany went east. Not till that flank was secured—a procedure which satisfied both the German and the Russian game—did Hitler attack in the west with what consequences we know to our cost; for only Dunkirk seemed to stand between him and complete victory. Having secured that flank in turn, convinced though he was that some time or other he would have to fight out the matter of colonial power with Britain, Hitler felt that for the moment it was too dangerous to attempt a move across the Channel. But, Britain being in his opinion no longer in a position to interfere, he decided to proceed against his most dangerous rival. Even up to that point he seemed to have hoped that in this adventure he could count on the British Government's hatred of Bolshevism to guarantee their non-interference while he fought the matter out with Soviet Russia.

It is to the eternal credit of Mr. Churchill and his collaborators that they saw through the ruse, and declared themselves on the side of Russia and of all those who were ready to fight Fascism. Such a turn of events not only took Hitler by surprise, but amazed Russia, who hitherto had not counted on such an open declaration. There are many who still believe, or affect to believe, that the course of the war in the year or so that followed, and the delay in opening the "Second Front", proves that Stalin was right in his tactics. They maintain that we would have left Russia to bleed to death, and to bleed Germany to death, before we would have risked active intervention in the west, if the Soviet Union had not taken the precaution of making sure that we were too deeply involved to withdraw, before it became involved itself.

However incomplete this analysis may be, there is, I believe, sufficient truth in it to establish two points:

1. That there is a real and irreconcilable antagonism be-

tween Fascism and Communism and that there can be no compromise between them. The totalitarian claims of each of them are bound to bring them into conflict.

2. That the Communist believes that, even though the course of the war drew together in an alliance against Hitler, for one reason or another, Soviet Russia and the capitalist imperialist nations, it was an uneasy and unnatural alliance.

In the opinion of the Communist the rulers of those nations are bound sooner or later to develop Fascist tendencies in some form or other, as they face their own inherent contradictions; they are so aware that at some period they must fight it out with Communism that they will use the peace to secure for themselves the most advantageous ground and conditions for that fight when it comes.

Seeing the situation in this black-and-white manner, and intent on exposing what he believes to be the real state of affairs, he attempts by his tactics to hasten the development of a clear left-right division, and to force the decision while the going is good. He sees in the intervention in Greece an attempt on the part of his enemies to hem him in; he sees in the Marshall Plan an effort to bolster up pseudo-social democracies to the same ends, and as jumping-off grounds for aggressive imperialism. How far that analysis of the situation on his part is an honest attempt to appraise the position is not in a sense important. It is decisive of his tactics, which have become quite clear. He must do all in his power to make social democracy unworkable, accentuate as far as possible the left-right divisions in the various working-class movements, and in the chaotic situation which results, build up a revolutionary force in each country which will see its only hope of salvation in a union with Soviet Russia, who will help it to seize power when the time is right.

These tactics are clearly visible in Europe to-day, and have been used in country after country in eastern Europe. They could be seen being used openly in France at the end of 1947. There, the inability of the social democratic forces to deal with a revolutionary situation seemed likely at one point to result in a victory for De Gaulle and a dictatorship of the right, which would in turn have forced many who had no particular desire for a Communist dictatorship of the left to choose that as the lesser of two evils. Whether or not De Gaulle is Fascist, he seems to be allowing himself to become the tool of the right, who, in face of the threat to their power, are forced to develop dictatorial and Fascist tendencies.

In between these comparatively small groups who know what is at stake, and who have a more or less clear policy to meet it, there lie the great mass of workers and lower middle class who are both the tools and the victims of the struggle. They have little understanding of the situation except where it affects them immediately and personally; but they are inevitably forced into one camp or the other by the sheer pressure of events on them. Whatever chance they have of uniting and controlling the situation vanishes once the revolutionary condition is reached. Their time for effective action lies in the period which precedes that. If they let slip that opportunity they are powerless to control the forces which soon reach demonic proportions.

But perhaps the nearest parallel to our British situation is Czechoslovakia. There the fear of the Soviet Union led the social democrats to isolate themselves more and more from their natural social allies in the west and inhibited them from building up a positive alternative to Communism. Coupled with this was a naïve trust in the pretence of the Communist that in a real social democracy he was prepared to subscribe to legal and parliamentary methods. This produced the expected result. It led to the inevitable overthrow of the social democrats by the Communist minority as soon as the latter was able to exploit the situation, and his establishment in power with the accompaniment of all the usual dictatorial methods.

The question, therefore, that we need to ask at this moment seems to me to be:

1. Is there any place in Europe where the conditions are

such that social democracy can carry through the revolutionary social and economic changes which are necessary to resolve the class struggle and lay the foundations of a new social order, which, while preserving all that is good in our western tradition, is in accordance with the demands which history now makes of us?

2. If there is, can these changes be made without resort to open violence and dictatorship?

3. Can they be carried through with sufficient speed to give hope to the social democratic forces in the rest of Europe, and to save them from an otherwise intolerable situation in which they will be forced to a violent upheaval and an acceptance of either Fascism or Communism against their will?

We are driven at once to consider the situation in our own country, the only one in Europe where, according to both Marx and Engels, "the inevitable social revolution might be effected entirely by peaceful and legal means".[1]

Has the war altered the situation in such a way as to give hope that this is now possible?

We have seen that the Communists have not only a clear-cut picture of the sort of world they are after, but that they insist that all tactics must be subordinated to the achievement of that end. They believe that they can mould people into the sort of persons that fit that world, and that in order to do so a dictatorship is necessary, wielded by those to whom this objective is perfectly clear, and who in their opinion can be trusted with unlimited power to gain that end. They assert that the end is so important, and the freedoms it will bring so obviously to be desired, that human beings must be prepared to forgo, for the sake of that end, certain freedoms now, to sacrifice themselves and to acquiesce in the sacrifice of others who will not willingly agree to this programme.

These tactics are only possible to people who have a certain view of the nature of human beings, their value, and their

[1] See above p. 125.

destiny. It is only because they have this view that they are able to bring themselves to regard the achievement of their utopia for hypothetical human beings not yet born as something so much more important than the welfare of millions now living, that the latter can legitimately be used as mere means to that end, and sacrificed to it.

Now, the British working-class movement started from a different angle. It did not begin with any blue-print of its aims, and it has had, for the greater part of its history, no clearly defined strategy for reaching even the vaguely defined ends that it set itself. The Industrial Revolution in Great Britain had already got well under way, and labour revolts had had a long history before Marx appeared. Although, therefore, he wrote on British soil, he appeared as an alien to a movement which had already not only some sort of shape to it, but a history from which it did not find it easy to dissociate itself. Though that movement has been influenced by ideas of a utopia, it did not start with any aim other than the ending of certain intolerable conditions to which its members were being subjected. Moreover, since it never had any philosophy of life other than the attenuated, but nevertheless real, one in the Christian world in which it had its own roots, it accepted quite naturally the view that no end in history was final; and that as far as men could see ahead, the things which they fought for were not ends at all, but means by which certain things which they desired could be achieved within their lifetime.

It was not, in fact, till after the 1914 war that the Labour Party—the official political instrument of the Labour movement—accepted Socialism as its official objective. Even when it did so, the Socialism which it accepted was interpenetrated all through with values which are bound up with the history of the struggle before Marx appeared on the scene. When it finally did accept Socialism it is true that parts of it accepted an interpretation both of history and of their immediate situation which had some resemblance to that advanced by Marx, for only so could they understand their situation and the part they must play in it; but they did so without adhering to the Communist philosophy of life and the tactics which followed from it. On the whole, it is true to say that they rejected all that conflicted with those liberal democratic premises which they still held subconsciously, and which they instinctively felt to be important in their human relationships.

The same is true of the history of the movement since that time. The British working man instinctively distrusts dictatorships, because experience has taught him that unlimited power tends to corrupt those who hold it, and he knows within himself that man is sinful and liable to corruption. He has an uneasy feeling that the use of unlimited power will not only lead to things in the interim which he hates, but that the sort of people which it breeds will in the long run so pervert the end that it will alter its whole character.

He could not, without a radical change of character, bring himself to do the sort of things which the Communist tactics demand. He could not ruthlessly liquidate his political opponents. He would never acquiesce in forced labour camps and other such drastic methods for dealing with the large number of persons who don't quite fit in with the tidy schemes. If his love of freedom leads him to reject totalitarianism as a means, that same love leads him to distrust Communism because he still links freedom with the right to such personal possessions as are not a danger to personal life, and, rightly or wrongly, he feels that Communism would deny them to him. With all his desire for a more just social order and his readiness to submit to certain disciplines for that end, the British working man is a confirmed individualist and a lover of freedom.

Thus, when at last the movement in Britain accepted Socialism, it did so still coloured with traditional liberal democratic ideas, with an insistence that at no point on the road should the treatment of persons conflict with those ideas. This insistence has coloured its strategy and tactics all through.

The British, as a people, appeal to ideas of right and wrong, and speak in the language of a nation which adheres to a common criterion for judging political issues because it holds a common philosophy of life. They have always been bothered, and sometimes inhibited in all sorts of ways, because of the demands which "minorities" made upon them. The rights of people to religious freedom, to free speech and free assembly have from time to time in the Labour Movement, as well as in all other political parties, altered the whole complexion of politics and political life, and that not only in its infancy, but right down to the present day.

What I am driving at is that all through we have been concerned primarily about persons: for freedom now for persons now living, because they have a right to it as persons; and that concern still colours all our tactics and strategy. Because we still think in these terms we have always distrusted utopias, though the movement has had its utopian phases. It has never allowed the utopian dream to become the criterion of present *ad hoc* judgements. The Communist would say that that has been our weakness. Yes, but it has also been our strength, for because of it we have weathered many storms which have split the movement into fragments in countries where the battle about absolute objectives has led to a complete division on immediate strategy and tactics. Here this "common sense" has won the day over and over again when a crisis threatened to produce a deadlock or a complete break with our traditions.

That this is still true of the movement can, I think, be made clear by three illustrations:

1. The Labour Movement believes that there is no way out of our present economic and social situation but by the use of the State machine to secure, for the community, control of the production of such things as the life of its members depends upon; and that there is no way by which men can be free so long as they are dependent for their livelihood on irresponsible power. Though it has come to the conclusion

that a planned society is the only way out of the chaos in the modern world, there is a general agreement that the principle must not be applied in such a way as to make life intolerable for persons now. Each particular thing to be brought under community ownership and control must be considered on its merits, and is to be taken over if, and at that point at which, the taking of it over conduces to the freedoms we desire within a measurable distance of time. It desires that, in the taking of them over, no real injustice shall be done to those who previously owned and controlled them, but that they shall be compensated for any real loss.

2. There is no agreed formula for the control of those things which are so taken over. The wide divergence of opinion which has always existed, from the pure collectivist to the guild socialist, still persists as to the amount of decentralisation which is desirable. The majority of persons in the movement, and its leadership, are agreed that there should be as much decentralisation and "workers' control" in industry as possible, because they are not concerned primarily for a mere efficiently run organisation, but for the rights and freedoms of the people engaged in the work. But it is indicative of the temper of the movement in this country that this matter will be settled by trial and error rather than by some rule of thumb method. Indeed, it is the power to control and use for community purposes that is felt to be important rather than the question of ownership.

3. At this particular moment the movement, and its leadership, is faced with problems which would be settled out of hand by the doctrinaire Communist, but which are not easy of solution to us, motivated as we are. We are faced, for instance, with a wave of Fascist and semi-Fascist anti-semitism, yet we are reluctant to pass a bill banning Fascist propaganda and Fascist meetings. It is interesting, too, that a short while ago a debate took place on the Stepney Borough Council on whether a Fascist book should be allowed in the Public Library. Now, I think it is fair to say that the Labour Movement hates Fascism and anti-semitism

as much as the Communist Party. The latter would ban Fascist meetings and Fascist propaganda of any sort without a discussion, and declares that the hesitancy on the part of the Labour Movement to do so is due to its sympathy with both. But the Labour Movement is reluctant to impose such a ban, not merely because it realises that once it gives way on such a matter of principle, its opponents, whether Communist or capitalist imperialist, may later use that as a precedent against itself, but because it instinctively thinks in terms of the right of the individual or the group to propagate its ideas, and sees in that right of individuals and of minorities the strength of a healthy society. It is, of course, possible that at some point the movement may be driven to impose such a ban, but it will do so with reluctance, and only when it is convinced beyond doubt that such a freedom is a positive danger to the freedom of others, and the danger so imminent that there is no other way of preserving that freedom.

It is an interesting comment on this situation that in Stepney the Communist Party have in 1948 won a local Borough Council by-election mainly by an appeal to the Jews in that area to vote for the Communist candidate on the ground that the Communists are the only bulwark against Fascism; quite openly playing on their fears of the "death cell" and horrors of Belsen. This quite unscrupulous use of racial fears to link the Jews to Communism is more likely to lead to an increase of Fascism than anything that has happened previously if the Jews yield to it, but it is consistent with the general Communist tactics.

We are led, then, to the conclusion that the Labour Movement is still inspired by a liberal democratic ideology, which has its roots in certain beliefs about man and the nature of life. Not about man in the abstract, but about persons now living. It has therefore an uneasy feeling that absorption in a blue-print of a future utopia, or the establishment of a dictatorship in order to achieve that pleasant objective, will so distort the characters of persons that life now will become unbearable, and that the means will so poison persons that the result will be problematical.

Notice I say that at some point the movement may be driven to action which seems to deny those values which appear to it now so vital. Realising this possibility, its members have never been ultra-critical of Soviet Russia, however much they have pointed to the things done by it which deny those values. They have felt that the possibility of a social revolution taking place in the west without violence is due to the fact that our conditions are not yet such that we have been forced by events to throw over those values which we hold dear, and that it is still possible for us to reach ends consistent with them without discarding them *en route*. If that is not so in large areas in Europe it is to be deplored; but it should not drive us into open opposition to those who have been forced into such a situation.

But that being so, the Communist Party in general, and the Soviet Union in particular, should have no real quarrel with us if in this situation we follow our natural line; and, moreover, if we seek co-operation with all those areas in Europe which are in a situation similar to our own, and with them seek immediate objectives consistent with those values, and leading in the direction of our more distant aims. But, whether they object or not, that is our programme, and nothing must deter us from carrying it out.

It is clear that it is the general desire of the Labour and Socialist Movement in Great Britain that, at every stage on the road towards the classless democratic society, it shall, as far as lies within its power, preserve those liberties which make real personal life possible for those engaged in the struggle. On this point there can be no compromise.

This concern for persons runs as a thread through the writings and speeches of the most representative of the leaders of the movement. Maurice Webb, for instance, writing in the *Tribune* (23rd January 1948), when he was Chairman of the Parliamentary Labour Party, said: "Does Socialism mean just a number of well-managed public utility companies showing a margin on the right side in their balance sheets, and kept in order by a handful of secretive, high-powered executives? If that's what you mean, you can count me out. I want public utilities and I want them well managed. . . . I don't mind your getting the best technicians to run them. But I will get fighting mad if you try to persuade me that, having got all that, you've given me Socialism. If that is your idea, you are doing something far worse than confusing means with ends (though you are doing that). You are prostituting the fine liberating idea of Socialism. You are using it merely as a device to get economic tidiness through managerial power. . . . I am a Socialist because I believe that the larger part of the business of getting a living can be separated entirely from what is called the price mechanism. I believe in the social distribution of available wealth according to needs. I want to see the social management of productive property so that all men may enjoy more private property. . . . I want to see the workers aspiring to wider spheres of responsibility than are now available to them. These are some of the things I mean by Socialism. And that is why I say that we have only made it possible by our measures of nationalisation. It is the final effect of public ownership in the homes and lives of the people that matters. Socialism must be made a living source of benefit and happiness to the nation."

This represents in my opinion the general outlook of the movement. But we are to-day in Great Britain in the middle of a struggle on this very point. There is a group in the movement, influenced by their interpretation—whether correct or not—of the teaching of Marx, which has already accepted, if not the complete Communist tactic, at least a philosophy of life which is bound, sooner or later, to lead to it. They help by their attitude to produce a situation in which that tactic may well become almost inevitable.

It is true to say that, generally speaking, that attitude is confined to those who have already accepted the Communist view of life and of man and who have rejected the

Christian view that man may not be used as a mere means to an end within history, but that opponents have rights and duties because they are persons, and matter as such. The vast majority, however, of persons within the movement still hold consciously or sub-consciously to the traditional view of man, and are uneasy about such a development. It is of the utmost importance that the movement in the west should remain true to this tradition, and not be unduly influenced by the completely different situation which prevails in eastern Europe, and the tactics which have resulted from it.

The difficulty is that the mass of our people, and many of our leaders, are not aware of the real nature of the issue. Instinctively they do as a rule the right thing, because they are that sort of people. But it is almost inevitable that they will lose the battle unless a greater number, both among the leaders and in the rank and file, are consciously aware of the integral relationship between theory and practice, between philosophy and action, between theology and life.

This battle will not be won unless we free ourselves from what Richard Crossman in the *New Statesman* (24th January 1948) calls "the Russian complex"—a complex which was fostered not only by the contemplation of the Russian "success", but by the continued failure of the movement during the inter-war years and what Crossman describes as "the Labour Movement's sense of exclusion from national affairs". But, as he goes on to say, "This sense of inferiority is fast vanishing. . . . Instead of unconsciously and out of weakness relying on another power to change the world for us, we have taken on the job ourselves. We no longer need the myth of Soviet Russia to compensate for our sense of frustration. But it is equally important that we should not replace it with an anti-communist myth. We should be strong enough and self-confident enough to-day to face the realities of Communism without the hysteria of the Red-baiter or the self-deception of the fellow traveller."

The fact that, at last, the British Labour Movement is freeing itself from the "Russian complex", and finds itself, at last, in a position to stand on its own feet and follow tactics which are in keeping with its traditions, leads me to believe that it is capable of offering to Europe a real alternative to Communism. But in order to understand why and how this alternative became possible, we must go on to examine the effects of the war on the movement, and on the British people generally.

7

SOCIALISM AND CHRISTIANITY IN BRITAIN

IN a previous chapter I attempted to outline the situation as I saw it in Great Britain up to 1939. There seemed then little hope that the Labour Movement would ever achieve political power. It made little impression on the technicians and the middle class, upon whom the application of so much of its programme depends. Some sections of it were being driven in desperation to accept a semi-communist philosophy and leadership.

The coming of the war altered that situation radically. It lifted the working class at once out of that awful trough of despair and made its members feel that they were persons again, with a real part to play in life. Now at last they were wanted. There was to be no more unemployment, no more feeling of uselessness and futility. They were wanted at last for a job that seemed well worth doing. Events now seemed to be justifying the stand they had been making for many years on the international front. They had hated Fascism, and during a long weary period they had watched it spread. In spite of their own sufferings they had been continuously protesting against this growing tyranny. Watching the thing grow—Japan, Germany, Spain—and the gradual gathering into its tentacles of country after country—Manchukuo, Abyssinia, Austria, Czechoslovakia—they had continued to protest to a people which seemed to be concerned only to keep the whole thing on somebody's else doorstep. But now at last the decision to fight had been made and they were wanted.

That first year—the "phoney year" as we called it—when nobody seemed to be capable of taking effective action as the German forces overran Poland, and we were engaged in the East End in sandbagging and endless disputes over air-raid shelters and such like problems, I need not dwell upon. But then came Dunkirk; and almost overnight something seemed to happen to us all. Mr. Churchill's call was an echo of that which we all felt. Just when Hitler thought we were dead, we came alive. Now at last we had a job to our hearts. Everything available was to be thrown in to face a common danger—all our energies, wits, resourcefulness, money. Nothing was to be withheld by a nation united against a common peril.

The story of our end of it has been told over and over again, and I don't want to repeat it here. But we lived, we lived again. Our houses might be destroyed, our belongings sacrificed, our lives in danger; but we lived because we were all conscious that we were doing something that had to be done, and the sacrifices we were making were not silly things inflicted on us, like going short of food and clothing and houses in a world of plenty, or unemployment and misery in a world where there were so many things which needed to be done. They were real sacrifices, not only asked of us, but demanded by us, in response to a real situation in which we were eager to play our part.

There were, of course, mistakes and disputes. Everybody makes mistakes and no government or people is perfect or ever will be. There were scroungers, looters, black-marketeers; but we saw them in proportion to the gigantic task we were all engaged on.

The men and women from another stratum of society who came down to do many jobs among us came now as friends to whom we could talk naturally and with whom we could work in comradeship; for they were in this struggle one with us. There was an absence of the usual sham in those new relationships; if they were sharing our struggle, they were sharing, too, our risks and were happy to do so. Many of them, like us, for the first time in their lives were learning what it was to do a job that brought unity to their lives. They were finding a comradeship which was richer than anything they had ever known.

It was out of that common life and comradeship that the post-war situation was born. The people who voted the Labour Government into power were those people who had been released from inhibitions of all sorts and who had learned the joy of a rich relationship with people from whom they had before been separated by artificial barriers. They were determined to carry that spirit and relationship into the post-war world, and the job of peace-making and reconstruction.

As a body, they rejected Mr. Churchill's leadership in that task, in spite of their great admiration for his leadership in war. They rejected it because, though they knew that there were few if any living men capable of such great leadership in a war in which he wholeheartedly believed and in which he so naturally voiced the common thought, they did not believe that his aim in this post-war task coincided with theirs. He was too deeply committed by his past record. The capacity for ruthlessness, which made him such a terribly efficient war leader, incapacitated him for an era of peace-making and reconstruction in which imperialism and dictatorship had no place; in which persons, and homes, and freedom, and individual responsibility had now to come into their proper place. Whether we were right or wrong, as a nation we rejected his leadership, and put our trust in a team, and a policy, which had been worked out in outline over years of struggle and suffering. We were not going to be wangled back to "1939 and all that".

But that policy was a living, malleable one, capable of adjustment to changing circumstances in response to human need. The great thing was that people saw in it a means of expressing in economic and social terms the vision of a new community life that had been opened by common work and suffering. The thing that mattered was the comradeship we had found, the release from fear and other inhibitions which war, with all its horrors, had given us, the crusade of liberation to which we were committed, and in which we were now joined by numbers of people who hitherto had not known us, but who had found us, and whom we had found, in those years of struggle.

The working-class movement in Britain had at last come into its own. It began as a great protest against tyranny and injustice, as a demand for freedom, and for the elementary rights of men and women and children to be persons and not slaves to things. It believed that things and processes ought to be controlled by persons responsible to a community of persons. It was never a merely class movement. For, though its strength naturally lay in the working-class organisations, its aim was a classless society and the elimination of the class war as a permanent feature of society. However much we might owe to Marxism, and we owed much, we were never Marxian in character.

If the decay of capitalism forced our organisations to adopt a defensive attitude, and to spend much energy in fighting to prevent the destruction of such gains in human rights as had been won during the heyday of British imperialism, we could not rest content with that position, but looked forward to the time when we could advance with a positive programme of Socialism. Moreover, we increasingly recognised that many of those gains, and our comparatively high standard of living, had been made possible only at the cost of the enslavement of others, and were never really happy about it. We sought to undo those wrongs; to set those people free who had suffered at our hands; and, turning from the defensive to the offensive, to use the whole strength of our movement in the struggle for community.

The war gave us our opportunity. It cleared the air. It brought to an end that era of fear and futility. It made not only possible, but imperative, a wholesale reorganisation of our domestic and international economy.

But it did more. It brought about something that Marx never thought possible. By itself the working-class movement can never carry through a peaceful revolution on the scale which is demanded, in a country where a large middle class exists, without the active help of that class. Whereas before the war on the whole that middle class was fearful of radical change and of working-class aims, the war had brought a new understanding and a desire for common action.

War is an evil thing. It is terrible that men should kill one another; that they should destroy so many things that they need for their livelihood; that, as a result, so many should starve and go short of the very necessities of life; but war does not come out of the blue. It is itself the consequence of what has gone before. It is the result of the sin and failure of man in his personal, social, and international life. But it is not just evil, any more than a bodily abscess is evil. It is the declaration of a hidden disease which demands a surgical operation—a bursting out which exposes the rot within—yet with all this, the offer of a new life.

All that I have written about is the consequence of the sin of man; the greed and apathy; pride and the love of men and women for power. It was not confined to Britain; the same symptoms were visible all over the world. It showed itself in the Far East, and in the ever-growing horrors and brutalities in central Europe. There was a time when, if men had repented, they could have done something about it; but they did not. The very sins which were the cause of it all continued to aggravate and spread the disease, as individuals and groups sought to save themselves at the expense of others, and to shut their eyes and ears to the sights and sounds of human suffering and the warnings of worse to come.

Internationally they tried to push the whole thing off on to somebody else's doorstep, but, instead of that, they saw it coming nearer and nearer, till it enveloped them. Nationally, they went on hoping that something would occur to right the situation at no cost to themselves. But there is no escape. There is a point at which powder fires; there is a point of tension at which a boil bursts; there is a point at which the unresolved conflicts in society break into the open and demand a decision. Whether that is good or bad depends on your point of view. To human beings in concentration camps suffering almost unendurably, and without hope of release, it is, indeed, welcomed as holding out at last the possibility of freedom. To those more comfortably situated, or hanging on by their teeth to the freedoms which still remain for them, and terrified of being involved in a situation which might endanger them still further, it may seem at first an occasion for despair. But, at least, it means that a new situation has arrived which forbids any longer an escape from responsible action. Now at last those who professed sympathy have to declare by deeds how real were their declarations.

The outbreak of war in this way does not mean that, even if the barbed wire which enclosed them is blasted, those who were before imprisoned are now going to be set free, for freedom is something positive. But it does mean that a new situation has arisen in which the question of freedom or slavery has a new context and a fresh possibility. At least those who have blown down the barbed wire are now inescapably involved in the issue. They can no longer avoid action of some sort, and that action will lay bare the value of their former pretensions.

The same thing holds true on what seems to be a purely material level. I have tried to give some idea of our terrible pre-war housing conditions in Stepney. They were the result of generations of sin and neglect. When the Labour Party at last took control at County Hall they found themselves in the position of wanting to rebuild the whole area, and of being prevented from doing so by the fact that there was little or no open ground on which to begin. The bombing blasted to pieces houses which had been condemned years before, and the pre-war Stepney was changed almost overnight. By circumstances outside our control whole areas were cleared, bug-ridden furniture burnt, and people scattered to the four winds of the land. These events made not only possible, but imperative, a complete replanning of the whole borough; and with it the possibility of relating it to those changes which had already come about, or which we desired to happen in our social life and habits, for we had now no alternative but to rebuild. Human beings, who before were passive victims of things and circumstances, were now free to plan and act as persons, and by their planning and action, by bricks and mortar, reveal the values they held.

We were not now faced with the question "Can we build or not?" but "How shall we build?" For build we must. The destruction cleared the ground literally, and made not only possible, but inevitable, a new Stepney. That Stepney may be better or it may be worse, but it will be a new one. There, at least, in one area, we were free to make choices; free to decide within certain limits what sort of Stepney we wanted. Even if freedom were limited to things like bricks and mortar, houses and flats, spaces and playgrounds, we had wide choices to make which inevitably reflected the ideas which men had about one another, about family life, about community, and, in general, about the sort of life that they wished to live.

But the time is short. This comparatively fluid situation is generally of brief duration and a few major decisions at the start soon begin to issue in a general pattern, which again tends to become set. The time factor in human affairs is an important one. I remember once, during the 1914 war, when I went before some high authority who had to decide whether or not I was a fit person to become a chaplain, one of the questions I was asked was what I would do if I saw a man lying on a battlefield with only two minutes to live. My reply was evidently not satisfactory, for my questioner proceeded at length to tell me what I ought to do and say, and finished by asking: "Now, don't you think that is what you ought to say?" My reply was: "Yes, but he's been dead just ten minutes."

Only too often in human affairs we are brought up against the fact that we are living in a world of time and space, and that "time marches on". Only too often we try to temporise, to put off the decisions; but our very temporising is, in fact, a decision which involves us in consequences. A few major decisions for better or for worse lay a pattern which again begins to grip us and determine our lives.

In this particular matter of bricks and mortar it is easy to see how once we have set about our task of building our houses and flats, community centres and what not, they are capable of but little alteration for generations. It was the Industrial Revolution and its aftermath which built Stepney as we knew it, and the sins of that age were reflected in it. We were caught up in that, and there was needed more than good will to break away from it. And that was true not only of our local situation, but of the wider life of which we were a part. It seemed to many of us in those years before the war that human beings had allowed themselves to be so much in the grip of circumstances that they were able to exert very little control over them. It explains in part that feeling of impotence which infected us all. It was as though some great inhuman, impersonal thing had us all in its grasp and was carrying us whither we knew not. We could only wait for what was "round the corner", hoping against hope that it was not to be worse than the present. We saw this thing, war, coming nearer and nearer. There were points at which the danger might have been arrested, but the decisions to make no decisions were decisive in determining its inevitability until at last it engulfed us, and miraculously set us free. It is one of the mysteries of history: a mystery which I believe is only explicable in terms of a living God active in history.

Every now and again, in the lives of nations, groups and individuals, caught up in the pattern of life which is the consequence of their sins and failures, and perhaps in particular of their pride which seeks to make a god of their successes, there comes a time when they become aware that the things in which they have put their trust are in danger of failing them and that a dreadful state threatens them. In terror they clutch their little world and their possessions still tighter and hope that it will pass them, while they hit out blindly against the unknown thing which threatens them. But there is no escape. Whether as, in the case of nations, it is war, or some revolutionary upheaval, or, as in that of individuals, a moral disaster, a clash of some sort becomes inevitable.

If it were possible for man indefinitely to continue in a way of life which contradicts certain simple, but fundamental, laws which govern life, there would be no hope. But it is not possible. There comes into the normal and expected run of man's affairs an inthrust which is revolutionary in the sense that it produces a new situation, in which there are vital elements unpredictable along the lines of the purely evolutionary development. It is no longer static and stagnant; it is fluid and moving. Men who before seemed tied and impotent are now not only forced to act and to make operative decisions, but have themselves been changed in character by being violently torn from their old alignments. But that fluid situation lasts for a comparatively short time. The decisions which man now makes, reflecting his present ideas about himself, his neighbour, his scale of values, and his conception of the purposes and ends of life, manifest themselves in the general pattern of life which he begins to build. Soon he is again caught up by that pattern, and carried along by it till the arrival of another crisis.

These crises are the decisive points in history. The limits of man's freedom are so conditioned that a determinist philosophy has arisen which concentrates his attention on the periods of bondage and ignores the crucial moments in the lives of individuals and nations which gave them birth. It is in such a fluid situation that we now find ourselves. Because of that fact the decisions which we now make have the utmost historical significance.

It is significant of this changed situation that the people of this country for the first time put into power a Labour Government. Those who desired a return to as much of the pre-war world as possible desired also the old Conservative Government. Had they succeeded we should now be facing a very different situation. It would anyway have been impossible for them to return to the old pattern. They would have been forced by the new circumstances to a continuation of some controls and a move in the direction of a more deliberately planned society. But there would have been a very different scale of priorities than those now operative. They would, I believe, have deferred schemes of social betterment, such as family allowances, improved old-age pension, the raising of the school-leaving age and extensions of holidays with pay. They would have cut food subsidies and wages, and already a queue would be forming at the Employment Exchanges, with unemployment to provide the incentive to work. Those who had the money, and nothing else better to do, would have been free to go abroad and spend unlimited money there; free to buy motor-cars and unlimited petrol; free to eat unlimited food in West End hotels and restaurants. The Government would have lifted restrictions in the building industry in order that those who had the money could spend it on building houses for themselves, or for sale to those who could afford to buy them; while those whose needs were the greatest would have been neglected.

That is, I believe, our experience of the sort of priorities the Conservatives believed in. That, too, is all we can gather from the negative criticisms voiced by their chief spokesman and from their lack of any positive programme. With that course of action at home there would have gone a continuance of the old imperialist policy, involving us in a renewal of the conflict with India, Burma and other spheres, and a common front with the most reactionary elements in America against Communism, resulting in an atom war on a gigantic scale. I don't believe that the Conservatives want these results, but they want something else so badly that they are prepared to "take the risk" of securing them, and to gamble on the consequences.

To those who think that that picture is overpainted I think it is necessary to point out that, however fluid the situation in which we find ourselves, however free we may feel ourselves to be, we are all of us, as individuals and groups, still very much conditioned, in our thinking and acting, by our past history. Unless we have not only rejected the philosophy and outlook which guided us in past situations, but positively embraced a new one, we naturally make the former the basis for our decisions in any new situation which confronts us. This double process is called "repentance". We are entitled to assume that any party which has in the past governed its political and social actions by a particular philosophy and outlook is most likely to continue to do so however radically the situation may change, unless it has given positive signs that it is repentant.

But it is equally significant that our people, while rejecting a return to "1939 and all that", emphatically rejected Communism. While there was a general desire to cement the friendship and new understanding with the Soviet Union which had grown up during the war, they showed clearly that they were determined to preserve all that was good in our native tradition. They naturally turned, therefore, to the company of those men and women who had slaved and suffered for generations, and who had been striving to build an organisation which should politically and economically lay the foundations of a new social order in order to express those ideas of justice and freedom consistent with their tradition.

It is to-day a matter for real thankfulness that at last, in our generation, that movement should receive this accession to its strength. The gap between the Labour Movement and the middle class has never been a wide one in this country. But before the war insecurity and the fear of unemployment among the middle classes themselves forced them more and more to adopt a defensive attitude. The war tore them from their moorings. It made it possible for them to think again and to do so more objectively.

The Labour Movement has always believed that political power must rest upon an economic foundation. But it has also always felt that there was something lacking in the movement until the manual workers were united with the "black-coated worker", the technician, and workers in every sphere of human activity, without whom any rich social life was inconceivable. Here in Stepney, when we talked of the future, we thought naturally in terms of a community of those who worked in dock and factory, at the bench and the desk, of clerks and social workers, doctors, parsons, nurses, and teachers: living together, working together; a mixed community of persons each bringing some contribution to a life rich in culture and experience. We have always felt that it was wrong that they should work with us or alongside us and yet live away from us, and we wanted to build a new Stepney in which this rich common life could flourish. Now at last the changed political and economic situation has made this possible. That statement is equally true of our whole national life.

It is important that we should all realise this vast change which has taken place in Britain, and should act accordingly. It means that there exists in this country, at the present time, a strong group of people who are prepared to go forward to the building of a new social order by peaceful and legal means, maintaining all that is best in our British tradition; prepared to discard all imperialistic aims and Fascist tendencies; while rejecting as inapplicable to our situation the tactics of Communism and the materialistic philosophy upon which they are based.

There exists at this moment no alternative to the Labour Party for the attainment of these objectives.

A government which attempted to force us back to the economic and social ideas current between the wars would, in my opinion, produce a situation which would bring speedily its complete antithesis through a bloody revolution. A Communist government could attain power only if the country as a whole had lost faith in our historic effort to settle our vast social problem without resort to civil war. It could rise to power only after a violent revolutionary struggle in which the workers were driven by fear and desperation to seize power. It was in such a situation in Russia that the Menshevik philosophy and tactics ceased to have relevance, and in which the Bolsheviks appeared to be the only people capable of creating, at a terrible cost, some order out of the chaos.

But we are not in such a situation. The Labour Party is in power to-day because the country, as a whole, has faith in the future, and does really desire a social order expressing more nearly those Christian, liberal, democratic ideas which have slowly taken root among us. It is precisely because we are not looking to the past, except as a guide to the future, and because we are not driven either by fear or despair, that we can adopt tactics consistent with the whole tradition and outlook that gave our movement its birth and cohesion.

It is, I believe, only in one particular historical situation that people with our outlook have the power to make this vast change in social relationships without a violent upheaval. It is that in which we now find ourselves. Those who know and want this way hold the reins of the political machine. The vast mass of workers by hand and brain are behind them, eager and capable of making political decisions effective in the realm of the political and industrial world. But for this sort of revolution to be successful the sacrifices which the situation demands must be offered willingly, not extorted from those called upon to make them.

Have we the will for such sacrifices? Make no mistake about it—they are very real ones. I believe that the reason why we have not yet been able to call them forth to a larger extent is that a great many people do not realise the manner and urgency of them, and that a great many others fear the consequences if they respond and others do not.

It is no less true of the working class than of other people that their mentality and general attitude to life is conditioned by their history, and, more immediately, by the history of the inter-war years. The failure on the part of many of our new friends, and by so many newspaper critics, to understand this, is to-day causing much confusion, and aggravating the trouble. They do not understand, either because they do not know, or because they have forgotten, the tragedy of those years. When, for instance, they read about certain restrictive practices in industry, or, say, the strike in the Grimethorpe colliery, they do not take into account the sufferings of these same men during that period, or realise that their attitude to-day is closely related to it.

I devoted so much space earlier in this book to a description of the conditions of a working-class area because I wanted to make our friends understand those years of semi-starvation, the hopelessness of the feeling of being unwanted, the desperation of the hunger-marchers, the fear of unemployment, the break-up of family life under the Means Test. If such things are difficult for our friends to grasp, how much more difficult for the indifferent who, looking back to what they call the "good old days", are unaware what bad old days they were to the masses. To those who do grasp that truth it is a matter for continuous marvel that the men and women who had so suffered could respond so magnificently to the necessities of the nation when war broke out. But the coming of peace brought to a tired people not only a longing for a little respite, but a resurgence of the fears that beset them in those evil years, and a determination to hold on to every safeguard against their return.

Some of my readers may remember the rise of Stakhanovism in Russia in 1935. It began when a worker named Stakhanov mined 102 tons of coal in one shift. It was obvious that special conditions and special tools had been provided to enable him to achieve this record. But it was the beginning of a movement which sought to make the pace of certain specialised workers under peculiar conditions the norm, and to dub as slackers those who could not maintain it. It is something like that which many people are now demanding of the workers in this country.

But they demand even more than that. They demand a

complete reorientation of the trade-union movement, without any realisation of the situation against which it has long struggled. For years the trade-union organisation has been concerned to safeguard the workers in steadily worsening conditions, and to prevent encroachments on their liberty. Every battle won had to be consolidated by some agreed formula, to which appeal could be made in times of attack. While there were some efforts at co-ordination by Transport House, the real struggle was carried on by the individual unions themselves, or by groups within the unions, who held their ground, or made advances and secured better wages and better working conditions, only in so far as they were in a position to demand and enforce them. Those wages and conditions had often no real relationship to the hardness of the work, the skill of the workers, or even to the priority of the work from a social point of view, in comparison with other jobs. They were secured and maintained either because the unions were able to enforce them at a time when the economic situation made the employers incapable of resisting, or because the possibility of financial gain in a particular commodity made it politic and profitable for the employers to grant them. Often men and women who were working for long hours at tedious and hard jobs were, and still are, the worst paid of the lot, simply because they had no power to enforce better conditions. At one time in our history it was the dockers living on an almost starvation wage, fighting for an extra bob a day. At another it was the agricultural workers, with a history stretching back to the Tolpuddle martyrs, fighting for the right to organise, contesting every inch of the ground as they advanced to conditions which were still pitiful when war broke out. At a third, it was the miners, resisting almost to blood, as they sought to safeguard themselves in a falling market; those who were still in work trying to hold the fort against better times, while thousands of their comrades were enduring semi-starvation in their derelict villages or scrounging in the streets of London for a living.

Practically every petty regulation and "restrictive practice" has a history, and to the worker concerned is the fruit of a bitter struggle; a thing of value for the safeguarding of his liberty and human rights in the future. The miners, who are asked now in peacetime to become almost Stakhanovites, are conscious that every bit of ground they give away, every extra foot of stint which they agree to work in this emergency, will be taken as the norm and enforced as the minimum if an unscrupulous and hostile government comes into power. The docker, who has by years of bitter struggle lifted himself out of degrading conditions of serfdom and misery, and has at last established himself as a person to be taken notice of and treated with respect, has hedged himself round with a whole network of defence which bristles with anomalies, but which is nevertheless important to him because each part of it is the fruit of bitter struggle. The bricklayer—now wanted desperately, then thrown on the slag-heap—has had to safeguard himself by laying down conditions which prevent the exploitation of the weaker by the enforcement, as a norm for all, of standards fixed by the capacity of the stronger workers.

Restrictive practices, ca-canny, the tale of bricks, the length of the stint—all these things are written in blood and tears. Any attempt by any government to tear up these agreements, so hardly won, would be resisted by the whole working class. Those who know how the workers have suffered know the reasons for that attitude. Even if a Labour Government is now in power, how long, they ask, is that to last? Even if the mines are nationalised, what guarantee have the miners that the new masters will not soon be the old under another name? Every point given away now will be used by an unscrupulous government later on as a precedent. For an outsider it may be easy to say: "Let every man give of his best, let the bricklayer lay as many bricks as he can, let the miner who is fit be the pace-maker for the slower ones! We need houses; we need coal; we need to train men in unlimited numbers; and we want each of them to go all out at his work and produce to his utmost capacity.'' It is easy to say that with no knowledge of the history of the working-class movement, or of the sufferings of those now called to such an all-out effort.

The men now called slackers for not responding to such a call cannot easily forget that the restrictions and union regulations, which they are now invited to cast aside, are things for which they have fought many a bitter battle in the past, and which, in times of slackness and unemployment, have alone stood between them and even worse conditions. To be sure there is a Labour Government; but what guarantee is there that it will continue to hold office, since its survival depends not only on the votes of the manual workers, but on the floating, and to the worker capricious, middle-class vote? To throw aside now the props which have been his mainstay in those hideous years, and for which he has fought so bitterly in the building up of his union, is, indeed, to make a great sacrifice, and to take a tremendous risk. Those who rail at the Labour Government for their failure to enforce hard conditions and to break long-established treaties—in fact, to govern with a big ''G''—do not realise the nature of the problem which confronts them. The working-class mind in Britain to-day is to a great extent the product of the history of capitalism and imperialism, both triumphant and in decay. The very things which seem a hindrance now are things which have kept alive the hope of the future; the fruits of many a battle won at the cost of great sacrifices. The workers naturally fear to let them go.

It is not a thing to be ashamed of, but a fact of which we may justly be proud, that when in the war it came to the test, the British working class held back nothing in a cause which they believed was a supreme struggle for national existence and for the safeguarding of human rights. The magnitude of the call brought a release from fear. But if war temporarily lifted that fear and gave back to the workers a measure of prosperity and of freedom they had not known for years, the coming of peace brought, with the hope of ermanently better things, the fear also of the old, and, with he fear, the holding tight to every safeguard. If that fear s intensified; if any serious attempt is made to force the vorkers back to those pre-war conditions, or to leave them lefenceless by forcibly depriving them of their safeguards gainst them; if the Labour Government fails, and, with the dvent of a Tory administration, large-scale unemployment egins again to rear its ugly head; if the situation which ollowed the last war and preceded 1926 begins again to levelop; and if the mass of workers in the country lose onfidence in the government of the day they will, I believe, ise in revolt, and we shall have to go through the horror f a bloody revolution.

My experience leads me to the conclusion that nothing vill drive the working class of Britain to endure again what hey then endured. They reached the limit of their capacity or suffering, and the threat of the recurrence of that suffering would be enough to ensure widespread resistance. Those vho wish to avoid that result and to win through to a eaceful solution of our present problems would do well to eflect on these facts. It would be something which, as I ave said before, would be foreign to our traditions as a ation. But we must beware of pride. If this is true of us, it s not because we are better than other men and nations. t is due to no such inherent goodness: but to God's providence, to our insular position, to the absence of foreign nvasions, to the "accident" that there is coal and iron in ur soil, and to the whole tactical position in the world in vhich those factors place us. We have not yet as a nation ither suffered as other nations have done nor lived so closely o the continuous fear of annihilation.

But in the world of to-day we are no longer insular; and ur test may come, not in the sharp, and comparatively hort, challenge of war, but in the long-drawn-out agony vhich has tried many other nations and laid low their pretensions. Let not the ostriches count too much on their uperficial understanding of history; history has a way of recoiling on the heads of those who rest complacently in a short view. I believe that it is possible for us to win through to a peaceful solution, but only if we are prepared willingly to pay the cost which will otherwise be inflicted on us against our will.

Facing that situation at home; facing a world in which the destruction had been terrible, with millions of people suffering and crying for help, a world complicated by the despair of further millions of displaced persons; coming into power in conditions hardly to be paralleled in history—the Labour Government felt compelled to play for time. It did so in order to secure for our people a breathing-space in which to make possible some adjustment in the minds of those who feared the return of "1939 and all that" as a living death.

Already, in order to win the war, we had put ourselves in pawn to America and used up the whole of our foreign reserves. We had now to call upon the U.S.A. for still further help, even though this was taken by a great many people as an indication that we had made the decision to cast in our lot with a new American imperialism in the dog-fight which seemed to be developing between them and the growing Soviet power in eastern Europe. At the moment of writing we are involved in the complications and the implications of the Marshall Plan. The need to safeguard our own standard of life, the much more pressing and immediate danger of starvation in Germany and elsewhere in Europe combined with the threat of a complete disintegration of social life in those countries, has made some such overall planning necessary. The U.S.A. has offered to provide the means by which much can be done in the direction which we all desire.

I believe that we should welcome this gesture and accept the help which is offered without feeling that we are thereby committing ourselves of necessity to the American way of life, just as I believe that we should welcome co-operation with the Soviet Union, whenever it is offered, without committing ourselves to theirs. In either case, of course, as indeed in our own desire to help in central Europe, such intentions are not entirely altruistic or disinterested. Rarely, if ever, is that or can that be true of nations.

But I believe that we must squarely face the fact that, whatever the U.S.A. or the Soviet Union may or may not do, we ourselves hold the key to the ultimate solution of the social problem which confronts us all alike. There is something in the British way of life and the British tradition which, though it came near to breaking-point at many stages in our capitalist and imperialist phase, has yet survived triumphantly, and is now seeking to redeem the past and witness to something which is neither American capitalist imperialism nor Communist totalitarianism. Standing firmly by our convictions, we must to-day boldly witness to that peculiar democratic Christian tradition which is the better way and the hope of the world. If we are true to ourselves we shall win through.

The time factor is important. It is now or never. But the ultimate solution lies, not with governments, but with persons. The Government must continue to work out a planned economy, and to see that more and more of those concerns which are vital to the life of the community are brought under community ownership and control. They must do all in their power to revive British agriculture, not only in order that we may be less dependent on others for our food, but in order to redress the balance in over-urbanised and over-machine-minded people. They must further develop and foster the growth of those natural groups and voluntary societies which are the strength of a real democracy. They alone are competent to deal with "spivs" and "drones" and to implement the Christian moral principle "if any will not work neither let him eat"—a Biblical injunction which, significantly, Communist writers still attribute to Karl Marx.

It is the Government's duty to see to it that the rank and file are kept fully informed of their plans, and to take them into their confidence as to why this or that thing is necessary.

They must help to build up at every level joint consultation committees, so as to give to those working in every department of life a greater sense of responsibility by entrusting to them more and more powers on the level which more intimately affects them. But if there is to be a real scale of priorities, and a direction of labour and capital consistent with it, side by side with this a movement must develop from below, of a kind to show that the rank and file are prepared to accept responsibility and are ready to make the sacrifices and to take the risks which the occasion demands. There must be a readiness to forgo privileges and to waive restrictions which were once relevant to a defensive warfare, but which now in the new phase which we have entered are actually harmful. Together there must be worked out a comprehensive wages policy which, while safeguarding the standard of life of the better-paid workers, is consistent with this movement towards community, has a nearer relationship to the nature of the job and breaks away from the old system of cut-throat competition. There must be a preparedness to move forward as a team, ready to work as we have never worked before and to cast aside everything which impedes our progress towards our immediate objectives.

Such a programme will not be carried through unless the manual workers are convinced that they can count on continuity. So long as they fear the defection of the middle class and others who have helped to put the Labour Government into power, they will refuse to allow their organisations to be transformed into bodies with creative community purposes.

There is a danger that many people, called upon to endure queues, and rationing, and certain positive restrictions on their liberties necessary in this difficult situation, will refuse to continue to support this community effort, however much we may point to the indisputable fact that such rationing means better clothes and a more equitable distribution of food, and that such restrictions bring a great deal more positive liberty to masses less fortunate than themselves. All sorts of bribes are dangled before their eyes by the Opposition, and the dangers of this programme multiplied. Many who are already showing signs of drifting are led to do so partly because they do not understand these fears of the manual workers, since they have not been through the same experiences, and partly because they have fears of their own which have never been properly appreciated. They are rightly not prepared to help in the consolidation of the working-class movement in the narrow sense of the word; but they are, and they have shown themselves, ready for a movement towards community. The narrow objective only intensifies their fear of being crushed between the hammer and the anvil of capitalist-working class struggles. The wider objective brings them in as partners in a movement which they understand, and in which they have shown themselves to be capable of immense sacrifices.

Both groups must therefore co-operate together more closely by joint consultation. In the factories and at the bench that co-operation and mutual understanding is growing. But a great many people are excluded from it by the very nature of their jobs and their lives. A great effort must be made by us all on village and borough level, in voluntary societies and social activities of all sorts, to come together and thrash out our difficulties and to learn to work together for our common objectives. Only so will the fears on both sides be dissipated.

I do not believe that our people will shrink from sacrifice if they are convinced that we all mean business. None of us engaged in this adventure have ever believed that any social order worth the building could either be built or maintained without continuous cost. We know that it must in some real measure reflect the sort of people who build it. We know that so long as we live within history there will always be a beyond to which we must reach; for no human society within history can be either perfect or static. We believe that far better material conditions than anything we have known are possible for us all, and that, with all the material resources at our disposal, there is no need for so much human suffering. But we know also that those material things are mere means to an end, and that the hate, pride, greed, and acquisitiveness which the old order helped to breed and foster, and which are in all of us to a degree, must give way to those qualities which cost us something, like fellowship, humility, and a readiness to forgive and be forgiven.

In the end our objective depends on persons, not on things. Our quarrel arose because persons were losing their significance and becoming the slaves of things. When we demanded "nationalisation" we did so because we could see no other way, in this complex world, of freeing persons from the domination of things and of irresponsible power. We persisted, in spite of the warnings that we were heading towards servility in an omnipotent state, because we trusted in the soundness and democratic "common sense" of our people. Well, the test has come. Will our people offer willingly the service which the occasion demands? That is the challenge. Now, it is for each one of us to prove whether or not we can stand up to it and come through triumphantly.

But there are three things that we need to keep in the forefront of our minds:

1. As a nation, more than once in our history, divided though we were on fundamental issues—and those divisions at times have been very deep—we were able to contribute something vital which saved the world from its worst excesses in a time of crisis. The capitalist imperialist himself, as I have already pointed out, brutal though he so often was, was prevented from some of his worst excesses of power by the fact that he was constantly being brought to book by his own Christian conscience and being convicted at the bar of public opinion which tended always to use the Christian tradition and values as its criterion. When the Marxian says "There is no God", the British working man, in whom natural religious truth has consistently remained, with little or no theology, with little or no love for the Church or

organised religion, still feels deep down in his bones in spite of his Marxian bias that a blow is being struck at something which is the foundation of whatever philosophy he has, and of whatever hopes for the future there might be. His reaction to the miners' crisis of 1926, and the Mosley crusade against the Jews, was instinctive. His reaction to the brutalities of Mussolini in Abyssinia and Spain was not based on any complete analysis of international politics, but on an instinctive sense of right and wrong, which sprang up into life when he was confronted with such inhuman treatment of persons. He was quicker to respond to the despairing cry of those in the concentration camps in Germany because he was living nearer to simple truth, unperplexed by the complexities of political and financial considerations, than many others in this country, who hesitated because there were other things competing for their loyalty.

With all our bickering and our real fights, in the deadly class struggle which has yet to be settled there is something which the majority of our people hold in common, or, perhaps more rightly, something which we have received in common from the past, which recurring crises brings into the open again and again. It is a fact that, deep down in our consciousness as a nation, we believe that a human being is not a thing, but a person, and that he is a person because he is a child of God. We have never been able to bring ourselves to an outright denial of the fact that this belief has substance, because Jesus Christ died on the Cross to save human beings, and because He is God.

I feel sure that our people felt instinctively that Fascism was destroying the roots upon which all their hopes depended—the value and significance of man—and regarded this attempt to treat persons as mere creatures of the State and race with all his rights and duties completely dependent on the capricious will of his fellow man, as the very devil. It is that same instinctive sense which makes us now determined to be no longer tools or mere pawns in a vast financial game. In that task we have, I feel sure, a great many more allies than we know; and though there are a great many others whose material interests will no doubt bring them into direct opposition to us, they know in their hearts that we are right. It is important that we should use the whole of these resources, and not needlessly antagonise this active or latent good will.

This does not mean watering down our programme, but it does mean that, at every point in the struggle, we should continue to treat persons as persons, however much we may come into conflict with them. Any group of people who attempt to persuade us to do otherwise is not on our side. Our objective is to see that things are made the servants of persons, and that industrial and social purposes are subject to, and answerable to, community. To lose sight of the nature of a person in the struggle is to destroy our aim.

2. In this struggle we cannot cut ourselves off from the people of other nations, nor can the battle be won in isolation from them. For that reason we wish to maintain friendly relationships with all of them who are of good will. In particular, we look to our leaders in Parliament to co-operate with all those who are trying to build democratic socialist states, and to encourage and foster every attempt to develop that democratic way of life which means so much to us. We look to them to carry on with renewed vigour the task, already begun, of transforming an empire into a commonwealth of free and self-governing peoples, or to grant freely, as in the case of Burma, independent sovereign status to such who desire it. We look to them to do all in their power to feed and care for those in central Europe, or elsewhere, who are in greatest need.

Only with such a policy can we hope to lay the foundation of a just and lasting peace between the nations of the world. All these things are of a piece with the spirit of our movement, which has always been international in its outlook.

3. But the realisation of these hopes at home and abroad depends upon the willingness of our people to do their part and to do it not by compulsion, but by free co-operation.

Either we are right in assuming that this is the real character of our movement, and that we are capable in this crisis of evoking this sort of response, or we shall fail. A social democracy cannot compel obedience in the way that a dictatorship must, nor can it rely on the compelling incentives of hunger, want or greed, which capitalist imperialism takes for granted. In some measure, of course, these remain, but a social democracy cannot succeed unless it is capable of substituting for these compulsions a social-mindedness in which self-interest is seen to achieve its fullest satisfaction by seeking the common good.

How far is it true that our movement is still fundamentally Christian in character?

While it is still true, in my opinion, of the older generation, it is becoming less and less true of that which is growing up. Even with the older generation we are carrying over as a liability those years of estrangement between the open avowal of belief in God and the holding of certain views about life which depend on that belief. This cannot continue long without real danger to our own health and that of our movement. Our criterion, our scale of values, our belief in the nature and purpose of man, are not based on mere pragmatic theory, but on a belief in a living God, worshipped and honoured for His own sake as the source and sustainer and Saviour of all life. If that goes, there goes with it very rapidly the whole standard of morals. Truth and justice and right human relationships begin to decay.

If that change has already begun to show itself in the younger generation it is greatly through the fault of their elders. A greater number than many people imagine have, I believe, a faith which, though they may not openly confess it, yet remains with many of its fruits as a stand-by in times of personal and public crises. It is hardly to be expected that the growing generation should still believe in a God whom so many of their parents have treated as a "useful extra", and never publicly acknowledged in their later years. That means depriving the children of something which has meant, and which still means, much to them. In addition to this the children have been only too often deprived, by circumstances outside the control of their parents, of many of those things which we prize—home, family life, the loyalty and comradeship of men and women engaged in a crusade in which they believe, and for which they have lived and suffered together.

Let me give an illustration. Some time ago I was asked by a magistrate in court to explain why so many lads were passing through his hands for one crime or another. Two of the boys before him at that moment were respectively 16 and 17. For the first ten years of their lives they had been brought up in such unemployed homes as those which I have previously described and subject to conditions which I believe did more to destroy family life in the East End than anything in our history. Then came the war. One of them had been evacuated four times and had been in six different schools, none of them for any long period. From the age of 10 to that of 15 they had known no real home life at all. For most of that time they were in London playing about on bomb-damaged sites with occasional days at school; at nightfall their parents automatically went to the shelter some distance away. In one case the home was made so uninhabitable by blast that the shelter was the only real home the boy had known for four years. They both left school and went to work hardly able to read or write, with no knowledge of God, with no experience of real home and family life, into a world where the moral standards were low, where they were regarded almost as "cissies" if they did not do some petty pilfering or looting; while their elders looked upon a little black-marketing as legitimate fun.

Is it any wonder that they themselves adopted this standard and regarded "being caught" as the only crime, and that the old "we and they" attitude to law and society in general became natural to them. Yet the majority of boys like this are friendly, pleasant to be with, and with real loyalties which often conflict surprisingly with their wider social conduct.

In 1941 a friend of mine gave me a small car to help in my work. Shortly afterwards my house was destroyed and I moved to a new one in another district. Since there was no garage I left my car in the yard. A few days later it vanished. By a devious route it was returned two days later, with the tank full of petrol and an apology: "We did not know it was yours." It turned out that, when my loss was known, some girls in a local club refused to dance with the boys who had taken it to "do a job" until they had returned it.

Their conduct on the whole is governed by these local loyalties; for there is generally no wider social loyalty or over-arching moral compulsion which they are ready to acknowledge. Many of them have adopted the general attitude of that of the boy who said of his promiscuous sexual intercourse: "She likes it; I like it. What's wrong with it?" Yet their standards and values are higher as individuals than when they are to be found in gangs or in public places. Somehow a "natural" goodness remains, which ceases to govern their conduct when they are caught up with a social group where the standard is normally lower.

But that readiness to subscribe to a lower standard in public than in private life is, I think, equally true of the older generation. In my experience workmen do better work alone than when they are with their mates; their conversation and attitude to life is sounder in private than in public life. That needs qualification, I know, for there is much evidence that already a new spirit is beginning to show itself. But I think that it is only too often true that a group of individuals will together conduct themselves in a way that each member would repudiate in his personal capacity.

It was, for instance, once true that many people went to church, and said their prayers, and professed a belief they did not hold for fear of what the neighbours would say if they did not. To-day a great many people do not go to church or say their prayers, and pretend a disbelief, for fear of what the neighbours would say if they were honest about it all. Perhaps it is better that way, but it isn't good enough, and that goes for so much else in our social life.

I believe that deep down there is still something sound in the common people of Britain. It is not too late to arrest the process of decay which is destructive of all social life. Nothing can destroy the lack of faith in one another, the subterfuges, the lies, the low standards of morals, the black-markets, the bad and shoddy work, the slackening on the job, the things which militate so much against all our hopes for the future and our present happiness, but a resolve on the part of those who hate these things privately to make a firm stand publicly for the things in which they do believe. Only too often we fail to do so because we fear what the next-door neighbour will say, when all the time he is as eager to do as we are, but fears our sneers.

If we will be true to the best that is in us we need have no fear. At this stage in our history our young people and the suffering millions of the world are calling to us to give them back a faith by which to live and on which they can build. For individuals and groups in this moment of crisis to adopt a defensive attitude, and hang on to the security they have temporarily achieved for themselves, is a sure way to defeat.

There can be no hope of peace in the world, and no security, unless we can fairly speedily produce a social order in western Europe which will effectively solve the basic material and social problems left us as a legacy of a capitalist imperialism which, in its death throes, has led us through two world wars and the horrors of Fascism; an order which, by the quality of its life, is effective as a challenge to any atheistic system.

Great Britain alone of the countries in western Europe is in a position to lead in this venture.

However wrong the Labour Party may seem to be on this or that particular issue, it is in general right in that which it has set out to do, and there is, in my opinion, no possible political alternative to it in existence.

A great many people will no doubt feel that they can and do accept its programme and the main ethical principles upon which it is based, but do not accept the theological implications which I have discussed. I must be forgiven if I continue to maintain that, in my opinion, such a position is untenable for long, and that those who hold it are really living on the capital of those who are publicly witnessing to their faith in a living God. But we have enough in common to work together to produce what T. S. Eliot calls a "Christian Society", even though we may not get much nearer in our lifetime to a "Society of Christians".

There are others who still call themselves Christians, but who for some reason or other have ceased to witness publicly to their faith. For those of them who have become alienated from the Church because of the sins of Christians—real or imagined—to maintain this quarrel now is to endanger the future of millions. We have a greater quarrel to face together. It is the "quarrel of God"; the quarrel against sin, as it shows itself in ourselves, our pettiness, our apathy, selfishness and pride; as it shows itself in a social order which crucifies Christ in the person of the poor and hungry, the imprisoned and displaced persons, all over the world. Taking our stand together in that dispute, we will need all our faith, all our courage, all the strength that fellowship in Him and with one another can give us.

To those who reject this constructive programme and dream of saving themselves by uniting in a "holy war" against Communism, I would add but this by way of warning. You may succeed by atom bombs in defeating the challenge of eastern Europe; you may succeed temporarily by a new alliance of the upper middle class and the capitalist imperialist, together with some working-class support secured through bribery and fear, in driving men and women back to the hovels from which they have issued in challenge; but it will be at the cost of the devastation of Europe and through incessant crises and wars and human suffering. You can but postpone the reckoning; for the challenge will come again and again with renewed vigour, until you have faced honestly the situation which forces that challenge into the open.

APPENDIX

Letter to "The Times", 21st December 1940

SIR,

The present evils in the world are due to the failure of nations and people to carry out the laws of God. No permanent peace is possible in Europe unless the principles of the Christian religion are made the foundation of national policy and of all social life. This involves regarding all nations as members of one family under the fatherhood of God.

We accept the five points of Pope Pius XII as carrying out this principle (see *The Pope's Five Peace Points*, pp. 13-16):

1. The assurance to all nations of their right to life and independence. The will of one nation to live must never mean the sentence of death passed upon another. When this equality of rights has been destroyed, attacked or threatened, order demands that reparation should be made, and the measure and extent of that reparation is determined, not by the sword nor by the arbitrary decision of self-interest, but by the rules of justice and reciprocal equity.

2. This requires that the nations be delivered from the slavery imposed upon them by the race for armaments and from the danger that material force, instead of serving to protect the right, may become an overbearing and tyrannical master. The order thus established requires a mutually agreed organic progressive disarmament, spiritual as well as material, and security for the effective implementing of such an agreement.

3. Some juridical institution which shall guarantee a loyal and faithful fulfilment of conditions agreed upon and which shall, in case of recognised need, revise and correct them.

4. The real needs and just demands of nations and populations and racial minorities to be adjusted as occasion may require, even where no strictly legal right can be established,

and a foundation of mutual confidence to be thus laid, whereby many incentives to violent action will be removed.

5. The development among peoples and their rulers of that sense of deep and keen responsibility which weighs human statutes according to the sacred and inviolable standards of the laws of God. They must hunger and thirst after justice and be guided by that universal love which is the compendium and most general expression of the Christian ideal.

With these basic principles for the ordering of international life we would associate five standards by which economic situations and proposals may be tested (see *The Churches Survey Their Task*, pp. 116-17):

1. Extreme inequality in wealth and possessions should be abolished.
2. Every child, regardless of race or class, should have equal opportunities of education suitable for the development of his peculiar capacities.
3. The family as a social unit must be safeguarded.
4. The sense of a Divine vocation must be restored to man's daily work.
5. The resources of the earth should be used as God's gift to the whole human race, and used with due consideration for the needs of the present and future generations.

We are confident that the principles which we have enumerated would be accepted by rulers and statesmen throughout the British Commonwealth of Nations and would be regarded as the true basis on which a lasting peace could be established.

(*Signed*) COSMO CANTUAR.
Archbishop of Canterbury.
A. CARDINAL HINSLEY,
Archbishop of Westminster.
WALTER H. ARMSTRONG,
Moderator of the Free Church Federal Council.
WM. EBOR.
Archbishop of York.